Prayers from Saint Paul

Prayers from Saint PAUL

edited by PAUL HILSDALE

SHEED AND WARD : : NEW YORK

A Word of Explanation

THIS BOOK BEGAN with the preparation of but one or two pages for a short conference on prayer. At the time, it seemed a rather obvious way of using scripture when praying, and I took it for granted that in the past many people had done exactly as I was doing.

Only later, when looking for a book with the tedious work of editing already done, did it begin to appear that there was no such thing. So I put together a few more prayers and showed them around. Invariably they elicited the surprised comment: "You mean no one has done anything like this before?"

Next thing to do was to study the various translations of the Bible, looking for one that was *both* intelligible and prayerful. At this point I consulted an eminent Roman Catholic theologian. His reaction, in brief: "This is a great idea. Why not use the Revised Standard Version?"

A leader in the ecumenical movement, he is vitally interested in getting a common scripture, acceptable to both Protestants and Catholics. A common book of scriptural prayers would, he thought, be at least a welcome step in this direction. Each of us, then, in the presence of God and in the silence of our hearts would be reminded frequently that our separated brethren honor the same scriptural text that we honor; that they have been redeemed by the same Christ who redeemed us; and that they can pray to the same Father in Heaven to whom we pray—and in the same words.

If a Protestant were to edit such a book, it would seem fitting that he choose a Catholic's translation. A Catholic, in turn, should consider using a Protestant version. It was this consideration that finally determined our selection—for the Revised Standard is a kind of compromise text that most Protestant denominations agree on.

It is not, however, the most legible or the easiest to understand. And it is our hope that these prayers will lead ever more people to turn to the epistles themselves, unsimplified, unabridged, and unedited. When they do so, therefore, if they are not already familiar with Paul's enigmatic style—and who is?—they would be well advised to select a more modern and more colloquial translation. For the important consideration always must be to enjoy and understand.

Most of us, I suppose, will simply open this book at random to pray. But for those who are better organized there are three separate indices at the end of the book. The first falls into two main groups: prayers for times of joy and prayers for times of sorrow or concern—with rather existential suggestions of what those times may be! The other two indices will commend themselves especially to people who are making a retreat or preparing some kind of scriptural service.

If this book of prayers from the Revised Standard Version is given a friendly welcome by the members of our tragically separated churches, then we will have the warm assurance of knowing that we are praying together—to the extent at least of reciting the very same prayer. And if we begin to pray *with* one another, we may soon find ourselves praying more effectively *for* one another.

This then is our hope: A book of prayers from St. Paul that is both scriptural and universal; a common fund of thought and word that may stimulate a common longing of the heart; a united prayer that may—in its own very limited way—hasten the re-formation of a united Christianity.

Paul Hilsdale
Loyola University of
Los Angeles

Contents

III. *Prayers from* Second Corinthians

Prayers from Saint Paul

Introduction

MANY PASSAGES in St. Paul's writings about God are so alive with his personally experienced awareness of his Lord and Creator that they are, in their own right, already prayers. In this book we have taken these natural prayers and made them more visible by transposing them into a different key, simply taking the words of St. Paul *about* God and writing them as words addressed *to* God.

The words, then, are always the words of Paul, the voice is the voice of the translator, and only the inflection and the transposition of person is that of the editor.

In *Corinthians,* for example, Paul describes the end of the world and our entrance into paradise:

> Then shall come to pass
> the saying that is written:
> "Death is swallowed up in victory" ...
> Thanks be to God
> who gives us the victory
> through our Lord Jesus Christ. (*I Cor. 15:54,57*)

In prayer we take the same words but address them directly to Christ:

Then shall come to pass
your saying *in scripture:*
"Death is swallowed up in victory" ...
Thanks be to *our Father in heaven*
who gives us the victory
through *you,* Lord Jesus Christ.

In other passages there is a change of mood and tense as well.
In *Thessalonians,* for instance, Paul writes in the indicative,
simply telling his converts what it was that motivated his work
among them:

For we never used words of flattery ...
We were ready to share with you
not only the gospel of God
but also our own selves. (*I Thes.* *2:5,8*)

Changing the tense (from past to present) and the mood (from
indicative to infinitive) creates a strong and vital prayer for all
who are devoting their lives to apostolic activities:

Oh, give us the honesty
never *to* use words of flattery ...
Teach us, rather, to share with *our brothers*
not only *your* gospel, O God,
but also our own selves.

At first it was planned to do as in these examples and to
italicize each of these incidental transpositions of person, tense,
and mood. But this proved rather confusing for the reader and
altogether too distracting for the pray-er. Moreover, since the

prayers run systematically through the New Testament, keeping close to the original order of the epistles, the inquisitive reader can easily check with the original and discover for himself how closely it corresponds to the prayer.

At times a word or two has been added to the text by way of clarification. At other times a word or phrase has been dropped where it impeded the natural flow of the prayer, but if more than two or three words are involved the omission is clearly indicated by ellipses.

Italics refer to words that are the editor's not St. Paul's. They may also, even without accompanying ellipses, bridge the thoughts of an omitted phrase or sentence.

Some of our prayers are addressed to God the Father, others to his Son, Jesus Christ. This leads to problems because St. Paul refers to the First Person of the Trinity simply as *Theos* (God). With the exception of *Rom. 9:5, Phil. 2:6,* and *Titus 2:13,* whenever he uses the word "God" he means "God the Father." In these prayers we have tried to obviate this confusion by giving a fuller, expanded translation of *Theos.* writing "your Father," or "God the Father," or "Father in Heaven," or some other equally explicit title. For example, when Paul writes to the Romans: "*God's* love has been poured into our hearts through the Holy Spirit . . . We were reconciled to *God* by the death of *His Son*" (*Rom. 5:5,10*); our prayer reads: "The love of *your Father* has been poured into our hearts through the Holy Spirit . . . We were reconciled to *the Father* by *your* death."

One advantage to this collection of prayers from St. Paul is the new, unexpected clarity they give the individual epistles from which they are taken. They provide a kind of distilled essence of St. Paul's thought—and a wonderfully intelligible

essence it proves to be once it has been separated out from the
more historically-conditioned debates and problems of the
early Church, and from the intricacies of Paul's hurried, disconnected style.

Those who are studying the epistles, therefore, could well
afford the frequent meditative reading of these prayers. They
are both nourishment and medicine: medicine to prevent class
study becoming a coldly cerebral, merely intellectual exercise,
and nourishment that will develop in mind and heart an ever
deeper appreciation of Christ and of the Christian community.

In recent years there has been a certain amount of discus-
sion about the fact that the most widely used of our liturgical
prayers belong to the Old not the New Testament. Writers
have suggested that it might be advisable to balance off the
Psalms with some more specifically Christian prayers. Could
this collection be the first step towards a solution of the problem: this method of selectively sifting Holy Writ so as to mine
and distill authentic prayers directly from the inspired text?

But the public use of prayers like these in church is not
our immediate aim. Here and now they are offered rather for
private reading and meditation. They seem to be especially
adapted to the needs of a person who is too busy and distracted,
or too tired and sleepy for strict meditation. The individual
lines, set in thought units, lend themselves perfectly to what
The Spiritual Exercises refer to as the Second Method or the
Third Method of prayer—"contemplating the meaning of each
word" or "measured rhythmical recitation."

Hopefully, those who have given up on meditation manuals
will find here something more to their taste in the unadorned
words of sacred scripture.

I. Prayers from *Romans*

PAUL'S LETTER to the Romans was projected as a kind of theological summary of Christian teaching: not, of course, a dispassionate *summa,* written in the cold, organized Greek categories of a Western theologian; but a deeply experienced, personal witness to Christ and the Christian faith.

One theme stands out above all others: Our salvation is God's work not man's. When all is counted up and added, it is not what man does that counts but what is done to him. Babylon and its aborted tower symbolizes for all times the powerlessness of human pride; failing in his attempt to scale the ramparts of heaven, man waits for Someone to come down from above. But he has to be on hand when God comes; he must be available when he is called; he must be receptive to the influx of Divine Life, as a light bulb is receptive to the light-giving flow of electrons.

Paul's word for this receptivity is "faith." It is faith, he says, and not the self-important observance of a religious law, that makes us pleasing in God's eyes. And here we had better repeat, underline, and restate the fact that our English translations are treacherous, that the original Hebrew-toned Greek word used by the Apostle means ever so much more than our deceptively simple word "faith." If this fact is missed, everything is missed. For Paul, "to believe" goes way beyond any coldly cerebral assent to the truth. And it means much more than mere trust and confidence. It is a full, existential experience of the whole personality. It is man's open acceptance in mind, heart, and action of God and his plan. More, it is the intense reality of what goes on in mind and heart when they are actuated by the divine inflow. As such, faith is man's heart-felt response to the truth of God and to his love; or better, *it is God's own knowledge* throbbing in man's receptive heart.

Against this idea of faith as an experienced presence of God in our souls, stands the Pauline idea of "works," or "works of the Law," as something exclusively human. The Christian life must find its fruition, of course, in works; but it is the divine component of these works—our faith—that counts, not their paltry human element. "The promise to Abraham and his descendants . . . did not come through the law," wrote St. Paul, "but through the righteousness of faith" (*Rom. 4:13*).

In summary, Paul's insistence in this letter on the primacy of faith and the relative uselessness of mere works reveals his own keen awareness of the presence of God in human affairs, and his intuitive understanding of the divine initiative in our salvation. It finds expression in passages of violent, Hebraic prose poetry, many of which fit quite naturally into our prayer form. So many, in fact, that there is at least one prayer for each of the letter's main topics. So it is that in a real but limited way the prayers in this chapter sum up the key ideas of the whole epistle—though, of course, they can never excuse us from actually reading it in the original.

After an introductory greeting and a reference to his credentials as an apostle (Prayer #1), Paul introduces his theme by pointing to the historical fact of man's failure to live up to the moral law (Prayer #2). Clearly, law is not enough. Something more is needed; call it "faith" if you will, or commitment to the truth, or the acceptance of Jesus Christ (Prayer #3).

It is Christ who is the source of our hope and strength (Prayer #4). He is the Second Adam in whom the human race has been recreated (Prayer #5). In turn, "I must consider myself dead to sin and alive to God my Father" (Prayer #6). Sin is a slavery. In contrast, our new life presents itself as an experience of liberty and joy; it is a "life in the Spirit" (Prayers #7 & 8). Come "tribulation, or distress, or persecution, or famine, or nakedness, or peril, or sword," who will now "separate us from the love of Christ?" (Prayer #9).

At this point an historical problem presents itself to Paul's mind: Where do the Jews fit into the new scheme? Once God's chosen people, they are now outside the Christian community. What is to be their destiny? (Prayers #10,11.)

With this subject, so close to his heart, Paul concludes the doctrinal section of his letter. These basic religious truths must now be applied to the practical problems of the Christians in Rome. There are still jealousies and petty rivalries among them. Could a better argument be found for harmony and mutual charity than the doctrine of our membership in the Body of Christ (Prayer #12)? Even the payment of taxes should be a Christian thing, a religious submission to those whose authority comes ultimately from God (Prayer #13).

The liberal-conservative debate extends apparently as far back as the first century! Paul sets down guidelines, therefore, of tolerance and mutual respect (Prayer #14). The epistle closes with Paul's own plans for the future, with a long list of

12

PRAYERS FROM ROMANS

persons to be greeted, and finally (Prayer #15) with a paean of praise to "the only wise God [to whom] be glory for evermore through Jesus Christ! Amen."

1. CALLED TO WHAT?

The divine call I have heard is not an invitation to wrap my soul in silver paper and preserve it "unsoiled" for heaven. No, I have been called—along with Paul—to bear witness to the Good News. It is my privilege as a parent to have the gospel as a blueprint while building a Christian home for my children. I am called to be an informed and active member of an informed and active church. I am to be the light of Christ in the wintry darkness of this world, his protective warmth against the damp chillness of its air.

Romans

1:1   Your servant, Lord Jesus Christ,
          I am called to be your apostle,
          set apart for the gospel of God
2   which your Father promised beforehand
          through his prophets in the holy scriptures.
          I am called to bring the "good news"
          of your life and death,
4   and of your resurrection from the dead,
          Jesus Christ our Lord.

5   It is through you
          I have received grace and apostleship.

6   *I have been* called to belong to you.
           May I now be given an increase of
7   grace and peace
           from your Father, our Father,
           and from you, Lord Jesus.

8   First, I thank my Father in heaven
           through you, Jesus Christ.
9   *I want to* serve with my spirit
           in your gospel ...
11   that I may impart to others some spiritual gift
           to strengthen them,
12   that we may be mutually encouraged
           by each other's faith ...

16   This gospel is the power of God
           for salvation ...
17   and in it the righteousness of your Father
           is revealed.

2. SO SURE OF OURSELVES

When it is my toes that are being stepped on, how quick am I to react: I've got a right to at least *some* respect and consideration! But from my side how thoughtlessly do I trample on the feelings of others. The patent inconsistency between what I demand of others and what I allow in myself should at least make me humble. But

no, I turn to a mechanical, external observance of the Christian
law, boast of it, tell myself how "religious" I am, close my eyes
to the higher law of love—substituting a self-confident legalism for
Christ-centered charity.

Romans

2:1   I have no excuse
Lord, help me to see
that when I judge another ... I condemn myself,
because I, the judge,
am doing the very same things
I complain of in my neighbor.

3   Do I suppose that when I judge others
for actions that are selfish and thoughtless
and yet do them myself,
I will escape your judgment, O God?
4   Do I presume
upon the riches
of your kindness and forbearance and patience?
Do I not know that your kindness
is meant to lead me to repentance? ...

6   You will render to every man
according to his works:
7   to those who by patience in well-doing
seek for glory and honor and immortality,
you will give eternal life.
8   But for those who ... do not obey the truth,
but obey wickedness,

there will be wrath and fury,
9   tribulation and distress. . . .

13   It is not the hearers of the law
          who are righteous before you, my God,
          but the doers of the law
          who will be justified . . .

17   We call ourselves *Christians*
          and we rely upon the law
          and boast of our relation to God.
18   *And we claim to* know your will
          and approve what is excellent,
          because we are instructed in the law.
19   Each of us is sure
          that he is a guide to the blind,
          a light to those who are in darkness,
20   a corrector of the foolish,
          a teacher of children,
          having in the law
          the embodiment of knowledge and truth—

21   We then who teach others,
          will we not teach ourselves?
          While we preach against stealing,
          do we steal?
22   We who say that one must not commit adultery,
          do we commit adultery? . . .
23   We who boast in the law,
          do we dishonor you, O God, by breaking the law?

With sorrow and shame I confess that
24   your name, O God,
        is blasphemed among the nations
        because of us.

3.   EXISTENTIAL FAITH

It is Christ who has called us. We cannot boast that we have worked
for our faith and earned it. We can only be grateful, and ever open
to the future advances of God's friendship. It is this openness of
mind and heart, this warm acceptance and full commitment to God,
that St. Paul calls "faith." And it is faith, not the self-satisfying observance of a religious law, that makes us pleasing in God's eyes.
So we must learn "to believe"—always according to the full, existential meaning of the original Hebrew-toned word. We must learn to
give much more than intellectual assent to Christ and his Church;
we must rediscover Abraham's open and full acceptance in mind,
heart, and action of God and his plan.

Romans

        Eternal Father, my God,
3:22   your righteousness comes
        through faith in Jesus Christ
        for all who *open themselves to you*
        in mind and heart.

23   All of us have sinned . . .
24   We are all justified by your grace as a gift,

through the redemption which is in Christ . . .
If it is a sheer gift,
27   then what becomes of our boasting?
It is excluded.
4:17   *You are the God* who gives life to the dead
and calls into existence
the things that do not exist.
18   In hope Abraham believed against hope
that he should become
the father of many nations . . .
19   He did not weaken in faith . . .
20   No distrust made him waver
concerning your promise, O God,
but he grew strong in his faith
as he gave glory to you,
21   fully convinced that you were able
to do what you had promised.
22   This is why his faith
was "reckoned to him as righteousness."

With your help, Lord, I too will believe—
committing myself in thought, love and action
24   to you who raised from the dead Jesus our Lord,
25   who was put to death
for our trespasses
and raised for our justification.

4. CONFIDENT IN HOPE

"God's love has been poured into our hearts through the Holy
Spirit, which has been given to us." Here in a nutshell is the
basic theology of the lay apostolate. Christianity is the pouring into
our hearts of the love of God. And the Spirit who pours this love *is*
himself the eternal Trinitarian love between Father and Son. To
the extent that we accept it, we can be made sharers in the dynamic
"love of God." But love is an outgoing thing. If it "has been poured
into" my heart, then it wants to go out from me to my neighbor. In
short, I have been initiated in a life that must be "apostolic" if it
is to remain truly Christian.

Romans

I firmly trust that soon
5:1   *we will* have peace
         with God our Father
         through you, our Lord Jesus Christ.
2   Through you we have obtained access
         to this grace
         in which we stand,
         and we rejoice
         in our hope of sharing the glory
         of your Father.

         And I pray for the grace
3   to rejoice even in our sufferings,
         knowing
         that suffering produces endurance,

4 and endurance produces character,
   and character produces hope;
5 and hope does not disappoint us,
   because the love of your Father
   has been poured into our hearts
   through the Holy Spirit.

   You redeemed us
6 while we were yet helpless. . . .
8 Your Father showed his love for us
   in that while we were yet sinners
   you died for us. . . .

10 While we were enemies
   we were reconciled to the Father
   by your death;
   much more, now that we are reconciled,
   shall we be saved
   by your life.

5. THE SECOND ADAM

Saint Paul is always keenly aware of the solidarity of mankind, of our deep spiritual dependence one upon another—a truth obscured for us nowadays by four centuries of exaggerated individualism. We can begin to rediscover this truth by meditating about our dependence-in-weakness upon the first Adam. This should lead us back to

a deeper awareness of our dependence-in-strength upon Christ and
upon our fellow Christians.

Romans

> *Selfishness, sin, and suffering*
> *are man's doing, not yours, O God.*

5:12   Sin came into the world through one man
        and death through sin,
        and so death spread to all men
        because all men sinned . . .

15   Many died through one man's trespass;
        But this, I firmly believe, is but a shadow
        of the great positive fact that
        the grace of one man—you, Lord Jesus Christ—
        has abounded for many.
16   And your free gift
        is not like the effect of that one man's sin.
        For the judgment following one trespass
        brought condemnation,
        but the free gift following many trespasses
        brings justification.

17   If, because of one man's trespass,
        death reigned through one man,
        much more
        will those who receive the abundance of grace
        and the free gift of righteousness
        reign in life
        through the one man

who came to redeem us:
You, my Lord and Savior, Jesus Christ.

19   By one man's disobedience
        many were made sinners,
        so by one man's obedience
        many will be made righteous. . . .

20   Where sin increased,
        grace abounded all the more,

21   so that, as sin reigned
        and brought death to body and soul,
        grace also might reign
        through righteousness,
        bringing eternal life
        through you, Jesus Christ our Lord.

6.   THE FULLNESS OF LIFE

To an Eastern audience the sacramental water of baptism brought to mind the life-giving waters of the Tigris and Euphrates and the green fertility spread by these waters over the parched sands of the desert. Baptism is a symbolic watering, a symbolic source of life. Paul's converts descended into the water and were buried in it, mystically sharing Christ's death and burial. Then they rose out of the water to be clothed in the white robes of a new life—visible members now of Christ's visible church. Today, with our awareness of symbolism blunted by technology, we have to depend more and more on prayer to kindle in our minds an understanding of the death we have died to sin, and of the new life that is within our grasp, thanks to our sharing in the resurrection of Christ, "baptized"—plunged by water or desire—into his now glorified, victorious existence.

Romans

6:2   How can I who died to sin
            still live in it?

3   Do I not know that all of us
            who have been *taken up*
            into you, O Christ, by baptism
            were baptized into your death?
4   I was buried, therefore, with you
            by baptism into death,
            so that as you were raised from the dead
            by the glory of your Father,
            I, too,
            might walk in newness of life.

5   If I have been united with you
            in a death like yours,
            I shall certainly be united with you
            in a resurrection like yours.

6   I know that my old self
            was crucified with you
            so that ... I might no longer
            be enslaved to sin ...
8   If I have died with you,
            I believe that I shall also live with you.

9   For I know that you
           being raised from the dead will never die again.

           Death no longer has dominion over you.
10   The death you died,
           you died to sin, once for all;
           but the life you live
           you live to God, your Father.

11   So also must I
           consider myself dead to sin
           and alive
           to God my Father
           in you, Christ Jesus.

7.   SLAVERY TO SIN

Personal experience of sin—of actually doing what my better self
rejects—proves how desperately I need to share in the strength of
Christ. At the "realest" and deepest core of my being I *want* to be
master of my ship and captain of my soul. The "real me" rejects sin
and longs for grace, love, and control. But in the midst of the gale,
when fear, anger, and passion are calling, my ears choose to listen
only to their siren voices, blocking out the "realer" and wiser direc-
tions of my conscience, of my essential self. *Of myself,* then, I do
not have the strength to do what I most really want to do. I am a
kind of spiritual madman. Who will free me from this madness?

Romans

Help me, O God, since
7:15   I do not understand my own actions.
         For I do not do what I want,
         but I do the very thing I hate.

18   I can will what is right,
         but I cannot do it.
19   For I do not do the good I want,
         but the evil I do not want
         is what I do.
20   Now if I do what I do not want,
         it is no longer I that do it,
         but sin which dwells within me.

21   *O my God, it seems to be almost* a law
         that when I want to do right,
         evil lies close at hand.
22   I delight in your divine law
         in my innermost self;
23   but I see in my members another law,
         at war with the law of my mind
         and making me captive
         to the law of sin
         which dwells in my members.

24   Wretched man that I am!
         Who will deliver me from this body of death?
         No one else than you, my Father in Heaven,
         through Jesus Christ our Lord.

8. LIBERTY AND LIFE

In the preceding prayer Paul meditated on the fact that Christ came to liberate us from our slavery under "the law of sin." But this was only a beginning; he has freed us *for something,* for a new life "in the Spirit." This is a technical phrase with Paul which if not carefully understood leads to the tragic but common impression that the dishes, the job, the students, the children, and all such material concerns are at odds with "the spiritual life." Strangely enough he means just the opposite: When he speaks of life "according to the flesh" he means living just for self, just for pleasure, living *without* any realistic commitment to the world and to the things of the world. And when he speaks of life "according to the Spirit" he means a life that is powered and motivated not by self, but by the Spirit whom Christ promised to send; a life patterned after Christ's own deep concern for his brethren; a life, therefore, of intensified commitment to this world and to all who are in it.

Romans

Eternal Father, I thank you with all my heart
8:2 *now that* the law of the Spirit of life
in Christ Jesus has set me free
from the law of sin and death.

3 For you have done what
mere advice, rules or command could not do:
Sending your own Son
in the likeness of sinful flesh
and as a sin offering,
You gave me the strength and the power
4 to walk not according to the flesh,
but according to the Spirit.

5   Those who live according to the flesh
     set their minds on the things of the flesh;
     but those who live according to the Spirit
     set their minds on the things of the Spirit.
6   To set our mind on the flesh is death,
     but to set our mind on the Spirit
     is life and peace.

7   *I know only too well that* the flesh
     is hostile to you, my God;
     it does not submit to your law.
     But if I am living in your friendship, then
9   I am not in the flesh,
     I am in the Spirit
     and your Spirit, O God, really dwells in me.

     You have given life to my soul,
     and I believe that at the end of time
     you will give eternal life even to my body.
11   You who raised Christ Jesus from the dead
     will give life to my mortal body also
     through your Spirit who dwells in me...
13   If I live according to the flesh
     I will die;
     but if by the Spirit
     I put to death the deeds of the body,
     I will live ...

15   I have not received the spirit of slavery
     to fall back into fear,

    but I have received the spirit of sonship.
    When I cry, "Abba! Father!"
16   it is the Spirit himself
    bearing witness with my spirit
    that I am your child, O God,
17   and if a child, then an heir too ...
    a fellow heir with Christ—

    provided I suffer with him
    in order that I may also
    be glorified with him.

9. HOPE AND COURAGE

Insecurity is a symptom of our age. Paradoxically man feels most
insecure in a world where for the first time in history he is in the
driver's seat, controlling nature instead of being controlled by it.
This fear and psychological anxiety, however, may well be salutary,
since it forces me to keep feeling around for the roots of my being
(May I find them eventually in "the divine milieu"). Man's life has
been called "a quest for meaning and certitude"; and Christianity,
when we do not shield ourselves against it, answers this basic quest.
It assures us that our life here below *has* meaning, and that we may
now move forward with hope, confidence, and courage.

Romans

 8:24 Hope that is seen
     is not hope. . . .

25   We hope for what we do not see,
        Help us, Lord, to wait for it
        with patience ...

28   Father in Heaven,
        I know that in everything
        you work *for the true good*
        of those who love you,
        who are called according to your purpose,
29   *whom you desire* to be conformed
        to the image of your Son
        in order that he might be the firstborn
        among many brethren. . .

31   If you, O God, are for us, who is against us?
32   You did not spare your own Son
        but gave him up for us all,
        will you not also
        give us all things with him?

        How secure I am in the love of your Son,
34   who died, who was raised from the dead,
        and who is now at your right hand,
        the hand of his Father.
35   Who shall separate us from the love of Christ?
        Shall tribulation,
        or distress, or persecution,
        or famine, or nakedness,
        or peril, or sword? ...

38   I am sure
        that neither death, nor life,
        nor angels, nor principalities,
        nor things present, nor things to come,
        nor powers,
39   nor height, nor depth,
        nor anything else in all creation,
        will be able to separate us
        from your love, O God,
        in Christ Jesus our Lord.

10. PRAYER FOR THE JEWS

Like his Master who wept open tears over the impending destruction of Jerusalem, Paul is often preoccupied with the fate of his
"kinsmen by race." In this prayer, where he talks about "the Gentiles," we speak in our own cause and say "*we* Gentiles." But when
he says "my brethren" or "my kinsmen" we have nothing to change,
for his brethren and kinsmen are most certainly our own brethren
and kinsmen. Thus Paul's prayer for his fellow Jews becomes our
prayer. And Christ's personal, intimate concern for them becomes
our own concern.

Romans

        Lord, I ask you to deepen my love and concern
9:2   *yet more, that I too may* have great sorrow
        and unceasing anguish in my heart,
3   for ... my brethren, my kinsmen, *the Jews.*

4   They are Israelites, and
         to them belong the sonship ...
         the giving of the law,
         the worship, and the promises;
5   to them belong the patriarchs,
         and of their race, according to the flesh,
         were you born, O Christ,
         who are God over all, blessed for ever.

10:1   *They are fully my* brethren.
         My heart's desire
         and my prayer to your Father for them
         is that they may be saved ...
2   They have a zeal for your Father,
         but it is not enlightened.
3   For, being ignorant of the righteousness
         that comes from him,
         and seeking to establish their own,
         they did not submit to *your revelation.*

12   *But in your eternal plan, Lord,* there is
         no distinction between Jew and Greek;
         the same Lord is Lord of all,
         and you bestow your riches
         on all who call upon you ...
14   But how are men to call upon you
         in whom they have not believed?
         And how are they to believe in you
         of whom they have never *really* heard? ...

11:1   Has your Father rejected his people?
          By no means . . .
11   Have they stumbled so as to fall?
          By no means!
          But through their trespass
          salvation has come to us, the Gentiles.
          Lord, teach us to be grateful
          for the legacy we have received from them.
12   *And help us to understand that* if their trespass
          means riches for the world,
          and if their failure
          means riches for the Gentiles,
          how much more
          will their full inclusion mean
          when they are united again to their
          Church and ours!

17   Some of the branches were broken off,
          and I, a wild olive shoot,
          have been grafted in their place
          to share the richness of the olive tree.
18   But I must not boast over the branches,
          pretending I have earned or merited
          the faith that has been given me.
          Lord, help me remember
          it is not I that support the root,
          but the root that supports me. . .

22   Your Father's kindness to me
          depends on my continuing in his kindness;

otherwise I too will be cut off.
And so it is, you have told me, for the Jews:
23   If they do not persist in their unbelief,
they will be grafted in,
for your Father has the power
to graft them in again.

24   For if I ... a wild olive, have been grafted,
contrary to nature,
into a cultivated olive tree,
how much more will these natural branches
be grafted back
into their own olive tree.
And I believe that in his own good time,
your Father will bring back his chosen people;
25   *but not* until the full number of the Gentiles
have come in.
26   And so all Israel will be saved.
Lord, may this day of fulfillment
be soon!

11. THE WISDOM AND
KNOWLEDGE OF GOD

This brief hymn of praise closes the doctrinal section of Paul's letter.
Always he enlightens our minds with the truths of God (doctrine)
before demanding specifics of action (morals). With Paul, therefore,
I want to meditate on the wisdom and knowledge of my Father in

heaven, on the long-suffering providence with which he watched over his chosen people, and on his loving concern for the whole human race, a concern made visible in the person of his Divine Son.

Romans

11:33   O the depth of your riches and wisdom
           and knowledge, O God!
           How unsearchable are your judgments
           and how inscrutable your ways!
34   For who has known your mind, O Lord,
           or who has been your counselor?

           Whatever made me think in proud stupidity
35   that I have given a gift to you
           and that on my own right I deserve
           to be repaid?

36   For from you
           and through you
           and to you are all things.
           To you, O God, be glory forever.
           Amen.

12.   CHRIST AND MY NEIGHBOR

Whatever my specialized role in the Church, it is part of a larger task to which we are all committed, that of diffusing Christ's love to a wider and wider circle of brethren: I am to "practice hospitality

[and even] bless those who persecute me." As always, Paul spends
less time on *what* we should be doing and more on the *why*. We
ought to be living dedicated lives *because* "we are one body in
Christ." Hence it is Christ's love that wants to flow through my
hands and Christ's blessing through my tongue—Christ's divine
will ennobling all the otherwise routine events of my daily life.
So each of us must perform his own task well, for it is Christ's
task.

Romans

12:2   *I realize, Lord, that I* must not
        be conformed to this world
        but be transformed
        by the renewal of my mind,
        till I begin to desire your will:
        what is good and acceptable and perfect. . . .

5   Though many,
        we are one body in you, O Christ;
        and you have assigned each of us
        a different role in this your body.
        Individually we are members one of another,
6   having gifts that differ
        according to the grace you have given to us.

        We ask for the wisdom to know our gifts,
        and to use them:
        When a man is in service
7   *show him how to be generous* in serving;
        when he teaches
        help him in his teaching;

8   if he has to exhort,
         it is you who must inspire the exhortation. ...

         When I do acts of mercy
         may it be with cheerfulness.
9   Let my love be genuine.
10   *Lord, help us to* love one another
         with brotherly affection,
         outdoing one another in showing honor,
11   never flagging in zeal,
         aglow with your Spirit,
         serving you, our Lord.

12   *Teach me how to* rejoice in hope,
         be patient in tribulation,
         be constant in prayer,
13   contribute to the needs of the brethren,
         practice hospitality,
14   bless those who persecute me—
         bless and not curse them!

         Make me sympathetic and sensitive,
15   *that I may* rejoice with those who rejoice,
         weep with those who weep,
16   and learn to live in harmony with others.

         Lord, I ask for the strength
17   to repay no one evil for evil ...
18   and, so far as it depends upon me,
         to live peaceably with all.

May I never avenge myself . . .
20   but if my enemy is hungry, feed him;
        if he is thirsty, give him drink . . .
21   and not be overcome by evil,
        but overcome evil with good.

13. TAXES ET CETERA

"The night," indeed "is far gone," and we are living in a world that
has drifted perilously from its moorings. Daily the Christianity of
my views—or the lack of it—is being tested. Taxes are one test.
Have I really tried to see them as a Christian should, as a way of
"paying all [men] their dues," as my way of sharing God's creation
with those who are more in need than myself—with my own fellow
citizens and with those of the hungry and struggling developing
nations? Again, how Christian is my attitude to legitimate authority? In short, is the love of my neighbor only a good intention, or is
it operative in the practical sphere of daily action?

Romans

13:1   *It is your will, Lord, that* every person
         be subject to the governing authorities.
         For there is no *genuine* authority
         except from you, our Father in heaven. . .
2   If I resist the authorities,
         I resist what you have appointed,
         providing—you do not have to remind me—
         that they do not command what is unjust.

5   Therefore I must be subject,
         not only to avoid your wrath,
         but also for the sake of conscience.

6   For the same reason I must pay taxes,
         for the authorities are your ministers, O God.
         For this reason you have instructed me
7   to pay all of them their dues:
         taxes to whom taxes are due,
         revenue to whom revenue is due,
         respect to whom respect is due,
         honor to whom honor is due.

8   *May I learn to* owe no one anything,
         except love . . .
         For You have made it clear that
         he who loves his neighbor
         has fulfilled the law . . .
9   and that all the commandments
         are summed up in this sentence:
         "You shall love your neighbor as yourself."

11   *Help me to realize, Lord,* what hour it is,
         how it is full time now
         for me to wake from sleep . . .
12   The night is far gone, the day is at hand.
         Help me then cast off the works of darkness
         and put on the armor of light.
13   Help me conduct myself becomingly
         as in the day,

not in revelling and drunkenness ...
not in quarreling and jealousy.
In other words, Eternal Father,
14   *help me* "put on the Lord Jesus Christ."

14.   TOLERANCE AND UNDERSTANDING

The early Christians were torn by a lack of sympathy and understanding between the "weak" and the "strong," between the more
conservative converts who felt themselves still bound by Jewish
ritual and diet, and the liberals who had broken completely with
traditional Jewish observances. For that matter, Christian liberty is
a master theme of this whole epistle to the Romans; still Paul
counsels love and patience for those who find change more difficult
and more threatening: "Let not him who eats [the liberal] despise
him who abstains, and let not him who abstains [the conservative]
pass judgment on him who eats." The "strong" may be right the-
oretically, he says, but in practice they should try to shock less and
to show greater consideration for their more timid brethren.

Romans

14:10   *Who am I to* pass judgment
             on my brother?
             Who am I to despise my brother?
             We shall all stand before the judgment seat
             of your Father in heaven ...
12   and each of us shall give account
             of himself.

Give me understanding, Lord, that I may
13   never put a stumbling block or hindrance
in the way of a brother.
Of itself, what I say and do
may be perfectly right and moral,
and still mislead a simple, trusting soul.

14   Thus, I know
and am persuaded in you, Lord Jesus,
that nothing is unclean itself;
but it is unclean
for any one who thinks it unclean.
15   If my brother is injured by what I eat,
I am no longer walking in love;
I am letting what in itself is legitimate
cause the ruin of one for whom you died . . .

17   Your kingdom, O God,
does not mean *rules of* food and drink,
but righteousness and peace
and joy in the Holy Spirit . . .
19   Let me then pursue what makes for peace
and for mutual upbuilding . . .

15:1   We who are strong
ought to bear with the failings
of the weak.
Help us, Lord, to concentrate less
2   on pleasing ourselves, *and more*
on pleasing our neighbor for his good.

5   May your eternal Father,
       God of steadfastness and encouragement,
       grant us to live in such harmony
       with one another,
       in accord with you, Christ Jesus,
6   that together we may with one voice
       bear witness to eternal goodness and joy.

15.   THE TASK BEFORE US

Coming to the end of his letter, Paul is reminded of God's un-
bounded patience, generosity, and love—that he of all people, who
was once a persecutor of the Church, should be called to bring to
the Gentiles the gospel, the life-giving good news of Christ. This
prayer is, of course, a prayer for ordained ministers of God. But at
a deeper level it expresses the gratitude and resolve of all whose
privilege it is to be possessed by the warm truth of the gospel, bear-
ing witness to the Light in a world that is growing daily more dark
and perilous.

Romans

15:13   Eternal Father, God of hope,
          fill us, *we pray,*
          with all joy and peace in believing,
          so that by the power of the Holy Spirit
          we may abound in hope.

15   *I owe so much to* the grace you have given me
          to be a minister of Christ Jesus

in the priestly service of the gospel ...

17 I have reason to be proud of my work
for you, my God ...

18 and of what your Son has wrought
through me ... by word and deed,

19 by the power of signs and wonders,
by the power of your Holy Spirit ...

20 It is my ambition to preach the gospel
not where Christ has already been named,

21 *but to those* who have never been told of him,
that they may understand
who have never *really* heard of him.

I depend on you, Father in heaven,
16:25 to strengthen me
according to the gospel
and the preaching of your Son, Jesus Christ.
May I be a not-too-unworthy witness
of the mystery
which was kept secret for long ages

26 but is now ... made known to all nations ...

27 To you, the only wise God,
be glory for evermore
through your Son, Jesus Christ!
Amen.

II. Prayers
from *First Corinthians*

"PRAYERS FROM *First Corinthians*" contain two of the Apostle's most frequently quoted flights of eloquence and emotion: His praise of charity (Prayer #38), and his description of the transforming glory that will come to our bodies at the end of the world (Prayer #39).

In God's strange providence, we might have been deprived of these two intense prayers had it not been for serious abuses among the Christians at Corinth. (1) The community was becoming fragmented by factions, and (2) some converts—not yet fully converted from pagan theology and Greek philosophy —were expressing doubts about the resurrection of the body.

This first letter to the Corinthians was written in 57 A.D. from Paul's current center of operations at Ephesus. A delegation had been sent from Corinth with definite questions for him to answer. For some time he had been concerned about the difficulties of their remaining fervent Christians in the licentious atmosphere of what was possibly the most "wide-open" city of Greece. Their questions, therefore, provided him with an opportunity to write an extended letter of encouragement and instruction.

After an introductory pat on the back (Prayer #16), Paul laments the divisions among the Corinthians (Prayers #17 to 25) and the moral disorders that have been reported to him (Prayers # 26, 27). It is in the first of these sections that we have his famous development of the paradox of the cross (Prayers #18, 19).

Beginning with Chapter 7 of the epistle, he turns to answering the Corinthians' questions about marriage and virginity (Prayers #27, 28); about meat that had been offered to idols (Prayer # 29); and about the qualifications of an apostle (Prayers #30 to 33).

Next he sets down regulations for the Christian liturgical assemblies: (A) How the women should dress: They are not to pray with heads uncovered, and if any are "disposed to be contentious" about this, let them know simply that "we recognize no other practice"! (B) How the *agape* is to be conducted so that it will provide a fitting setting for the Eucharist (Prayers #34, 35), and (C) What is to be done about the gifts of the Holy Spirit (Prayers #36 to 38). It is in this section that he develops the idea of our membership in the body of Christ and of charity, or love, which is the bond of its internal union.

The fourth and final section is concerned with the resurrection (A) of Christ (Prayers # 39 to 41), and (B) of all Christians (Prayer #42).

16.   RICHES THAT SATISFY

That I have been born in a Christian land and in a Christian home is God's doing, not mine. That "I have been enriched" in Christ is a present from my Father in heaven. Now that I have received in the person of his Divine Son the pledge of his abiding love, I know that he will be "faithful to his promise." And I am assured that he will protect me and guide my path and "sustain me to the end."

1 Cor.

1:4   I give thanks
to my Father in heaven always
because of that grace of his
which was given me
in you, Christ Jesus.

5   In every way
I have been enriched in you ...

7   I wait for your revealing *at the end of time*
my Lord Jesus Christ.

8   You will sustain me to the end.
And I bask in the secure knowledge that

9   your Father is faithful,
by whom I have been called
in the fellowship of you his Son,
Jesus Christ our Lord.

17. I AM ASHAMED

The new faith of the Corinthians was still in competition with their old pagan habits. Some already were boosting their own "parish," their own organization, their own favorite group above all others. "I am for Paul, I am for Apollos, I am for Cephas." Alas, such parochial, jingoistic attitudes have not all been exorcised and banished by the Apostle's anxious rebuke.

I Cor.

1:10   Lord Jesus Christ,
           we ask for tact and patience,
           that all of us may agree
           and that there be no dissensions among us,
           that we be united
           in the same mind and the same judgment.

           I am ashamed, Lord, to admit
11   that there is quarreling among us . . .
12   One of us says: "I belong to *this movement*"
           or "I belong to *that one,*"
           "I belong to *this sect*"
           or "I belong to *a rival one.*"

13   But are you divided, O Christ?
           Was *it just a sect that was* crucified for us?
           Or were we baptized
           in the name of *a mere movement?*

18.   THE SHADOW OF GOD'S WISDOM

The wisdom of Christ makes foolish the self-styled wisdom of this
world. In the blazing light of Divine Truth what are all "the wise
men, the scribes, and the debaters of this age"? Is it possible that
some of the eternal wisdom which they have lost has come even to
me—to be possessed by one who is so small among men, so unedu-
cated and insignificant? And if so, what am I doing with this

treasure? What ever made the eternal God decide to use "the folly of what I preach to save those who believe"?

I Cor.

1:17   You have sent me . . .
         to preach the gospel,
         and not with eloquent wisdom,
         lest your cross
         be emptied of its power.

18   *Alas, to some,* the word of the cross
         is folly . . .
         but to us who are being saved
         it is your divine power.

19   For it is written:
         "I will destroy the wisdom of the wise,
         and the cleverness of the clever."
20   Where is the wise man?
         Where, *I ask myself, Lord,* is the scribe?
         Where is the debater of this age?
         Have you not made foolish
21   the wisdom of the world. For . . . the world
         did not know you through wisdom.

         And now you would use a foolish thing,
         my words, my life, and my example,
         and through the folly of what I preach
         save those who believe.

22   *Some* demand signs and *others* seek wisdom
23   but I preach you, Christ crucified,
        a stumbling block to *many*
        and folly to *many more.*
24   But to those who are called . . . you are
        the power of God and his wisdom.

25   For your foolishness, O God,
        is wiser than men,
        and your weakness, my God,
        is stronger than men.

19.   EVEN ME

Clearly the Father is not dependent on mere human talent, for he
has chosen such clumsy people to work with his Son for the salvation of the world. But he knows what he is doing; so I must be
confident that—if I let him—he will help even me acquire whatever
wisdom and holiness the job demands.

I Cor.

1:26   Not many of us are wise
        according to worldly standards,
        not many powerful,
        not many of noble birth.

27   You have chosen what is foolish in the world
        to shame the wise;

You have chosen what is weak in the world
to shame the strong;

28   You have chosen what is low
and despised in the world,
even things that are not,
even me ...

And you have made it perfectly clear
29   that no human being
might boast in your presence, O God.

30   You are the source
of my life in Christ Jesus—
Christ, whom you made our wisdom,
our righteousness
and sanctification and redemption.

31   *Teach me the lesson* as it is written:
"Let him who boasts,
boast in the Lord."

20.   EYE HAS NOT SEEN

Without the reassuring light of divine revelation, primitive man
wandered in search of a vague goal, struggling with uncertain fears
and hopes. How different, how sure, and how full of joy, therefore,
ought to be my Christian approach to life!

I Cor.

What you offer me, O God,

2:6   is not a wisdom of this age,
or of the rulers of this age
who are doomed to pass away;

7   but a secret and hidden wisdom
which you, Eternal Father, decreed
before the ages ...

9   No eye has seen,
nor ear heard,
nor the heart of man conceived,
what you have prepared
for those who love you.

10   You have revealed to us
through the Spirit
your great love and eternal providence.

12   We have received
not the spirit of the world,
but the Spirit which is from you,
that we might understand
the gifts you have bestowed on us.

21.   IN GOD'S NURSERY

God has given me a ray of uncreated truth to light my path and the
touch of his hand to strengthen me; but I am still weak, and I still
forget what I am about. I begin to rely on mere human standards
and natural reasons, then I find myself unable to understand the
truths taught by the Spirit. I must learn more and more to look at
life with God's eyes. Only to the extent that I do, will I be able to
work with others effectively in his cause.

I Cor.

Without your special light and strength, O God,
2:*14*   I cannot receive the gifts of your Spirit.
They seem like mere folly to me,
and I am not able to understand them
because they are spiritual.

Looking back at my life I see that at first
3:*1*   you could not address me as a spiritual man,
but only as a man of flesh,
as a babe in Christ.
2   You fed me with milk, not solid food;
for I was not ready for it.

And even now I am not ready,
3   and I am still of the flesh.
For there is jealousy and strife among us,
and I am behaving like
any mere ordinary man.

22.   THE FOUNDATION IS LAID

I have been born into a going culture. God's plan for the world is
moving forward in this family, this school, this country, and this
Church. If it is a good work, it was begun with God's blessing and
his grace. I cannot afford to forget that his supporting power is
equally needed now to continue the work and bring it to completion.

I Cor.

> *What have I to boast of? I am*
> *but the inheritor of countless generations.*

3:6 Some planted and *others* watered;
>   but it is you, O God, who gave the growth.

7   Neither he who plants, nor he who waters
>   is anything,
>   but only you who give the growth.

8   He who plants and he who waters
>   are equal,
>   and each shall receive his wages
>   according to his labor.

9   We are fellow workmen with you, O God.
>   We are your field, your building.

> *The Apostles*
10   according to the commission you gave them,
>   like skilled master builders, laid a foundation ...
>   Each of us *must now* take care
>   how he builds upon it.

11   No other foundation can anyone lay
         than that which is laid,
         which is your divine Son, Jesus Christ.

12   Now *it is our turn to* build on the foundation
         with gold, silver, precious stones,
         wood, hay, or stubble . . .

13   and fire will test what sort of work
         each one of us has done.

14   If the work which I have built on the foundation
         survives,
         I will receive a reward.

15   If my work is burned up, I will suffer loss.
         Grant, Lord, that my building
         stand firm and imperishable.

23.   TEMPLES OF THE HOLY SPIRIT

If we could only recognize the nothingness, the utter hollowness of
our lives. But the more hollow a chalice, the more it can be filled
with wine. True prayer should lead us towards a fuller understanding of the infinity that is poured forth in the souls of those who
recognize their emptiness. The next step will be love and gratitude
to the Spirit whose presence fills our mere human tents (in Hebrew,
"tabernacles"), transforming them into temples of the Divine.

I Cor.

         Help me, O God, to understand
3:16   that I am your temple,

and that your Spirit dwells in me.

17   If I destroy your temple,
you will destroy me,
for your temple is holy . . .

21   All things are mine,

22   whether Paul or Apollos or Cephas
or the world
or life or death
or the present or the future,
all are mine;

23   and I am Christ's
and Christ is yours, Eternal Father.

24. HOLLOW BOASTING

The existence of factions, of in-group and out-group, among the Christians of Corinth revealed the disruptive fact that even in things of the spirit individuals were boasting of special graces and setting themselves above others. But how could they—and how can I—really feel proud of things we could never have gotten all by ourselves, of things God has freely chosen to give us?

I Cor.

4:1   We are your servants, O Christ,
and stewards of the mysteries of God . . .

2   It is required of stewards
           that they be found trustworthy.
           Meanwhile I can see into my own heart,
           but not into my neighbor's. So I must
5   not pronounce judgment before the time,
           before you come, O Lord,
           and bring to light
           the things now hidden in darkness,
           and disclose the purposes of the heart.
           Then every man
           will receive his commendation from your Father.

           Teach me not to go around belittling my neighbor,
6   puffed up ... one against another ...
7   What have I that I did not receive?
           If then I received it,
           why do I boast as if it were not a gift?

25.   APOSTLE AND FOOL

Our Lord never promised his friends a thick bank roll and a good press. Quite the opposite. But for those who go all the way with him, he does guarantee a life of significance and inner contentment. May we learn how to accept graciously both the bitter and the sweet that he has in store for us.

I Cor.

4:8   Already others are filled!
        Already they have become rich! ...

9   I think that you have *deliberately*
        placed us, your apostles, last of all,
        like men sentenced to death.
        We have become a spectacle
        to the world, to angels, and to men.

10   We are fools for your sake,
        but others are "wise"...
        We are weak, but they are strong.
        They are held in honor, but we in disrepute ...

11   We hunger and thirst.
        We are ill-clad and buffeted and homeless ...

12   When reviled,
        help us to forgive and to bless;
        when persecuted, to endure;

13   When slandered,
        Lord, show us how to conciliate.

26.   LIBERTY IN CHRIST

Paul never presented Christianity as a series of commandments. Essentially it is a new life, a life in the Spirit. And the commandments are not tiresome, restrictive regulations, imposed from above. Rather, they are—if we could really understand them—rational conclusions that spell out the way any normal person *would want to live* if he realized the new life that is welling up within him.

I Cor.

You have made it abundantly clear, Lord,
6:9   that the unrighteous will not inherit
        your Father's kingdom . . .
        Neither adulterers nor homosexuals,
10   nor thieves, nor the greedy, nor drunkards . . .
        will inherit the kingdom of God.
11   Such were some of us *and with shame*
        I confess that such was I too.
        But we have been washed;
        we were sanctified and justified
        in your name, O Lord Jesus Christ,
        and in your Holy Spirit.

        From now on, with your help, Lord,
12   I will not be enslaved by anything . . .
13   My body is not meant for immorality
        but for you, my Lord. . . .

14   Your Father raised you, Lord,
        and he will also raise us up by his power . . .
15   For our bodies
        are your members, O Christ.
        And I would defile your love,
        were I to take your members
        and make them members of a prostitute.

        Teach me to remember, Lord,
19   that my body is a temple
        of your Holy Spirit within me . . .

I am not my own:
20   I was bought with a price,
         and now I pray that I will always
         glorify your Father in my body.

27. MARRIAGE LAWS

The Church in Corinth had written for Paul's advice on a number
of specific problems that were in dispute there. Here, then, he turns
to "the matters about which you wrote." The following introductory
words about Christian marriage give only what seems to be the
universally applicable section of Paul's complex advice to the Corinthians. The selection was not made, however, on the basis of mere
personal preference. In the introduction to the prayer that follows,
an effort has been made to justify it, pointing out that Paul's advice
at this point seems to have been given in view of his own and his
hearers' expectation of an almost immediate end of the world. So it
is probable that some of his advice would have been quite different
were he writing today. With this in mind, we have simply omitted
from the following two prayers most of those sentences that Paul
would probably have wanted revised and adapted to the needs of
his modern readers.

I Cor.

7:7   Each of us
          has his own special gift
          from you, our God,
          one of one kind and one of another.

10   *For those of us who are* married,
        you give charge, Lord, that the wife
        should not separate from her husband.

11   But if she does, *you wish her*
        to remain single or else be reconciled.
        And the husband should not divorce his wife.
        We really want to be obedient, Lord,
        but sometimes it is so very difficult!
        How desperately we need your help and
        encouragement.

28. CONCERN FOR GOD AND FAMILY

First Corinthians is one of Paul's earlier letters, and it seems that he
had not yet arrived at a fully personal understanding of Christ's
teaching about the Second Coming. If so, then this letter's advice not
to get married is to be understood in the light of the then-popular
belief that the end of the world was just around the corner. Paul
states honestly enough that "concerning the unmarried I have no
command of the Lord"; that he is giving only what he holds to be
the best counsel "in view of the present distress." Precisely in view
of this distress—in view of the heartbreak and turmoil that will ac-
company the final cataclysm—his advice is about the same as we
would give in war time to a boy who had been ordered away to
active duty. If this be the correct interpretation, then it is mainly
because "the appointed time has grown very short" that a man
should not burden himself with the added anxiety of "how to please
his wife." Would St. Paul give the same advice today in view of the
radically different conditions of modern life? The whole question is

exceedingly complicated, but as yet there is not enough evidence to
prove the oft-repeated view that Paul is here teaching the unquali-
fied superiority of virginity over marriage. Controversy aside, the
following prayer is at least a salutary reminder to married and unmarried alike, that in all our words and works we should be concerned less about our own ease and more about the love of Christ. In
short, what we need is a change of attitude not a change of state.

I Cor.

7:29   The appointed time has grown very short.
From now on,
let those of us who have wives
live as though we had none,
30   and those who mourn
as though we were not mourning.
Those of us who rejoice
ask your vision to see beyond our rejoicing;
and those of us who buy
pray that we be not enslaved by possession.

31   The form of this world
is passing away,
and, Lord, I so much want to be free
from anxieties ...

32   The unmarried man
is anxious about the affairs of God,
how to please you, his Lord.
33   But the married man
is anxious about worldly affairs,

how to please his wife,
34   and his interests are divided.

And the unmarried woman . . .
is anxious about the affairs of her Lord,
how to be holy in body and spirit.

But for myself, wherever I am,
whatever I'm doing, help me give
35   my undivided devotion
to you, O Lord.

29. LIBERTY AND ITS LIMITS

In the market at Corinth they sold meat butchered from animals
that had been sacrificed in pagan liturgies. Could the Christians buy
it or not? The more conservative, legal-minded converts from Juda-
ism said, "No." The liberals said, "Yes." So the problem was re-
ferred to Paul. The principles, he wrote back, are clear: The food is
not defiled for *there are no pagan deities* to defile it. Meat is meat,
and it is all fit for a Christian's table. *But* a naked principle—
"knowledge"—is not enough. More important for the Corinthians is
a charity that would bow before the delicate, if misinformed, con-
sciences of their more timid co-religionists.

1 Cor.

8:1   *Lord, help me to see how* "knowledge"
puffs up,
while love builds up;

2   *and keep me from* imagining that I know something,
when I do not yet know as I ought.

3   *For only* if I love you, O God,
can I be known by you.

    By themselves,

8   *mere external acts of devotion* will not
commend us to you, O God.
We are no worse off if we do not eat,
and no better off if we do.
You came to make us free,
to give us liberty of spirit, to rescue us
from a narrow, legalistic mentality.

    But you must help us be prudent, as well,

9   lest this liberty of ours
somehow become a stumbling block
to the weak.

10   For if anyone sees me, "a man of knowledge,"
doing what I know is allowed,
but what he thinks to be sinful
might he not be encouraged,
if his conscience is weak,
to do the same thing, subjectively committing a sin?

11   And so by my knowledge
this weak man would be destroyed,
this brother
for whom you died, O Lord Jesus Christ.

12   Thus by sinning against my brothers

and wounding their conscience when it is weak
I sin against you, O Lord.
So now with your grace,
I am resolved to try to think ahead
to the consequences of my actions,
and nevermore to be a cause
of my brother's falling.

30.   MONEY

Paul never apologized for talking money; he was much too aware of our solidarity in Christ, of our interdependence one upon another, of all the different ways we are able to share in the world-wide work of the Lord. He himself spent much of his time collecting for the impoverished Church in Jerusalem. If he were alive today he would, no doubt, be collecting for the interracial apostolate, for Latin America, for Community Chest, and for the United Nations. It is time for each of us to reflect prayerfully on the "talents" —both economic and spiritual—that God has entrusted to our care. Just how have we been using our money, our time, and our personal abilities?

I Cor.

Lord, if I cannot serve you directly
in the work of your Church;
then let me serve indirectly: serving you
in those who are full-time apostolic workers.

9:4   Do they not have the right
to their food and drink? ...

7   Who serves as a soldier at his own expense?
Who plants a vineyard
without eating any of its fruit?
Who tends a flock
without getting some of the milk? ...

9   It is written in the law of Moses:
"You shall not muzzle an ox
when it is treading out the grain."
Is it for oxen that you are concerned? ...

10   No, it is written for our sake,
because the plowman should plow in hope,
and the thresher thresh
in hope of a share in the crop.

And now your co-workers, my fellow Christians,
11   have sown spiritual good among us;
is it too much
if they reap our material benefits?

31. THE SELF-DENYING APOSTLE

A question for those of us who are engaged full-time in the active
apostolate, who are "professionally holy": How much do we do that
is *really gratis,* that is not "in our contract"? How well do our actions give the lie to cynics who see cheap self-seeking in every face?
Paul took no credit for preaching the good news, (his Christian
job). What he did credit himself with, and boast of, was the fact

that he did more than he had to (preaching *gratis*—teaching without remuneration and supporting himself after hours by the work of his own hands).

I Cor.

> *When I ask the people for support*
> *I am well within my rights,*

9:14 for you commanded that those who proclaim the gospel
should get their living by the gospel.

15 But *do I want to make* use of these rights? ...

16 If I preach the gospel
that gives me no ground for boasting.
For necessity is laid upon me.
Woe to me if I do not preach the gospel ...

17 I am entrusted with a commission.

> *But I would be specially deserving*

18 if in my preaching
I *proclaimed the good news* free of charge,
not making full use of my right in the gospel.

> *With your help, O Lord, I want*

19 to make myself a slave to all,
that I might win the more.

20 To the Jews I *propose to* become as a Jew,
in order to win Jews ...
To those under the law

I will become as one under the law . . .
21   To those outside the law
I will become as one outside the law . . .
22   To the weak I will become weak,
that I might win the weak.
Help me, Lord, to
become all things to all men.

32.   THE COURSE OF VICTORY

Memory fades and imagination deceives us. We pray, therefore, for clarity of vision. And we ask that the sun of God's Truth continue to shine upon the distant horizon where already we can see in outline the shape of our eternal goal. We may then be able to push towards it with ever renewed eagerness, determination, and vigor.

I Cor.

I have so much to do, Lord, if only
9:23   *I could* do it all for the sake of the gospel,
that I might share in its blessings.
14   I know that in a race
all the runners compete,
but only one receives the prize.
Help me so to run that I may obtain it.

25   Every athlete
exercises self-control in all things.

They do it to receive a perishable wreath,
but I *am promised one that is* imperishable.

26   I must not run aimlessly;
          I will not box as one beating the air;
27   but I will pommel my body
          and *with your help, Lord, I will* subdue it,
          lest after preaching to others
          I myself
          should be disqualified.

33.   OVERCONFIDENCE

The Israelites knew they were God's Chosen People. They shared in
the temple worship and were more or less faithful to all the external
observances of religion. But salvation demands more than this; it demands a constancy of love as well. Again and again, therefore, it
was just when they felt most sure of themselves that they fell. May
I learn once and for all not to put my trust in the externals of religious practice. May I learn never to be sure of myself—but always
sure of God.

I Cor.

          The ways you dealt with the Chosen People
10:6   *were meant as* warnings for us,
            not to desire evil as they did.

          I am not to be an idolater
          as some of them were . . .

8   I must not indulge in immorality
          as some of them did,
          and twenty-three thousand fell in a single day . . .

10   nor grumble as some of them did
          and were destroyed by the Destroyer.

11   Now these things, *you have told me,*
          happened to them as a warning,
          and were written down for our instruction.

12   *You were cautioning anyone* who thinks he stands
          to take heed lest he fall . . .

13   You are faithful, my God, *and I pray*
          with full confidence in your goodness
          that you will not let me be tempted
          beyond my strength.
          But with the temptation,
          you will also provide the way of escape
          that I may be able to endure it.

34. GOD AND NEIGHBOR

In the Christian Banquet we are united to Christ through the Eucharist. We are united also to one another. May this union persist for the rest of the day and the week, making us ever more conscious of "the good of our neighbor"—hence of God's glory—in our eating, our drinking, and in all that we do.

1 Cor.

10:16   The cup of blessing which we bless,
is it not a participation
in your blood, O Christ?
The bread which we break,
is it not a participation
in your body?

17   Because there is one loaf,
we who are many are one body,
for we all partake of the same loaf.

24   *And so it is your will that* no one of us
seek our own good,
but the good of our neighbor . . .

31   So whether I eat
or drink,
or whatever I do,
may I learn to do all to the glory of God,

32   and to give no offense . . . to your church.

33   *May I* try to please all men
in everything I do,
not seeking my own advantage,
but that of many, that they may be saved.

11:1   *In short, may I* be an imitator of Paul,
as he was of you, O Christ.

35.   THIS IS MY BODY

In early apostolic times the Eucharist was received at the *agape,* the community love feast. But these dinners at Corinth were marred by factions, with divisions developing between one group and another, between rich and poor, between the well fed and the hungry. It seems that they—like ourselves—realized only imperfectly the nature of the sacrament that Christ founded at the Last Supper. If we are to think less of the accidentals that separate us, we will have to concentrate in prayer on the great mystery of our supernatural unity— with the body and blood of the Lord making us one with him and one with one another.

I Cor.

Lord, I confess in sorrow and shame
11:18   *that often* when we assemble as a church,
there are divisions among us ...
20   *So that* when we meet together,
it is not *really* your supper that we eat
for we do not have enough love in our hearts.

23   *The account that Paul* received from you, Lord,
which he also delivered to us,
is that on the night you were betrayed
you took bread
24   and when you had given thanks,
you broke it, and said:
"This is my body
which is for you.
Do this in remembrance of me."

25   In the same way also the cup,
           after supper, saying:
           "This cup is the new covenant in my blood.
           Do this, as often as you drink it,
           in remembrance of me."
26   For as often as we eat this bread
           and drink the cup,
           we proclaim your death, O Lord, until you come.

27   Whoever, therefore, eats the bread
           or drinks your cup
           in an unworthy manner
           will be guilty of profaning
           your body and blood.
28   *Help me, then, to* examine myself,
           and so eat of the bread and drink of the cup,
           that I may be made worthy to become
           one with you and one with my neighbor.

36. A VARIETY OF GIFTS

In an age of specialization and division of labor, an insistence on the *different* gifts of the Holy Spirit is even more needed than it was in apostolic times. May we be granted the wisdom to recognize our own special competence and its limitations. And may this lead us to bury all big red jealousies, and even our little green envies.

I Cor.

12:4 There are varieties of gifts,
    but the same Spirit.

5   And there are varieties of service,
    but *it is always you whom we serve.*

6   And there are varieties of working,
    but it is the same God who inspires them all.

   To each of us is given
   The manifestation of your Spirit
   for the common good.

8   To one is given through your Spirit
   the utterance of wisdom,
   and to another the utterance of knowledge
   according to your same Spirit,

9   to another faith by the same Spirit,
   to another gifts of healing . . .

10   to another the working of miracles . . .

11   All these are inspired
   by one and the same Spirit
   who comes to us through you, O Lord,
   and who apportions to each of us individually
   as he wills.

37.   STATUS SEEKING

If the Holy Spirit has given us different spiritual gifts it is to build up the body of Christ, which is his church. And if Christ is to redeem and remake this world of ours, his body must begin to function as a well-coordinated unit. Pastors must learn to rely on and make use of the talents of their parishioners. Husbands and wives must learn to respect their partners and defer to one another's competence. Finally we must all put aside our petty status seeking and learn to find a higher fulfillment in the role that has been marked out for us individually by God.

I Cor.

12:12   The body is one
         and has many members,
         and all the members of the body,
         though many, are one body.
         So it is with you, O Christ.

13   For by one Spirit
         we were all baptized into one body—
         Jews or Greeks, slaves or free ...

15   If the foot should say:
         "Because I am not a hand,
         I do not belong to the body,"
         that would not make it any less
         a part of the body.

16   And if the ear should say:
         "Because I am not an eye,
         I do not belong to the body,"

that would not make it
any less a part of the body.

*Lord, help me to learn this lesson
once and for all!*

17   If the whole body were an eye,
where would be the hearing?
If the whole body were an ear,
where would be the sense of smell?

18   But as it is, your Father
arranged the organs in the body,
each one of them as he chose ...

21   So the eye cannot say to the hand,
"I have no need of you,"
nor again the head to the feet:
"I have no need of you."

22   On the contrary,
the parts of the body
which seem to be weaker
are indispensable,

23   and those parts of the body
which we think less honorable
we invest with the greater honor ...

24   Your Father has so adjusted the body ...
25   that there may be no discord in it,
but that the members
may have the same care for one another.

26   If one member suffers, all suffer together;
if one member is honored, all rejoice together.

27   Now we are your body, O Christ,
        and individually members of it.

28   And your Father has appointed in the church
        first apostles, then prophets, teachers . . .
        helpers, administrators *and all varieties*
        of ministries and occupations. Help us,
        we pray, to carry out our responsibilities
        always with alacrity and joy.

38. WHEN KNOWLEDGE
IS SWEPT AWAY

To be a Christian I must recognize and use the special abilities the
Holy Spirit has given me. And I must do so as a member of Christ's
body, coordinating my talents with those of my brethren—that the
world-wide work of Christ be not impeded by internal malfunction
and friction. Summed up in a word, I must have love.

1 Cor.

13:1   If I speak in the tongues
        of men and of angels,
        but have not love,
        I am a noisy gong or a clanging cymbal.

2   And if I have prophetic powers,
        and understand all mysteries
        and all knowledge,
        and if I have all faith

so as to remove mountains,
but have not love,
I am nothing.

3   If I give away all I have,
and if I deliver my body to be burned,
but have not love,
I gain nothing.

4   Love is patient and kind;
love is not jealous
or boastful;
5   it is not arrogant or rude.
Love does not insist on its own way;
it is not irritable or resentful;
6   it does not rejoice at wrong,
but rejoices in the right.
7   Love bears all things, believes all things,
hopes all things, endures all things.
O Lord, how far I am from this goal!

8   Love never ends.
As for prophecy, it will pass away ...
knowledge, too, will pass away.
9   For our knowledge, *you have assured me,*
is imperfect and our prophecy is imperfect;
10   but when the perfect comes,
the imperfect will pass away.
11   When I was a child, I spoke like a child,
I thought like a child,
I reasoned like a child;

but when I became a man,
I gave up childish ways.

12   Now we see in a mirror dimly,
but then face to face.
Now I know in part;
then I shall understand fully,
even as I have been fully understood.

13   So faith, hope, love
abide,
these three;
but the greatest of these
is love.

39. AT THE HEART OF THE GOSPEL

The Gospel, the Good News, is not a long series of rules and regulations. Our allegiance is not to a rule book or to a set of syllogisms; it is to the person of Christ, living and triumphant. This is "the gospel which we have received, in which we stand."

I Cor.

    Lord, that I may witness to the Good News
    in all its original purity and strength,
15:1   the gospel which we have received,
    in which we stand,
2   and by which we are saved . . .

3   For Paul delivered to us ...
     what he also received;
     that you, Christ, died for our sins
     in accordance with the scriptures,
4   that you were buried,
     that you were raised on the third day
     in accordance with the scriptures,
5   and that you appeared to Cephas,
     then to the twelve.
6   Then you appeared
     to more than five hundred brethren ...
7   Then to James, then to all the apostles.
8   Last of all, "as to one untimely born,"
     you appeared also to Paul.

9   *Yet he felt so keenly that he was* unfit
     to be called an apostle,
     because he persecuted your church.
     So how can I, who am still little more
     than dead weight in the church,
     feel so independent and self-assured?
10   But by your grace I am what I am,
     and your grace towards me was not in vain:
     For I have worked *for you—*
     though it was not I
     but your grace, O God,
     that worked within me and bore fruit.

40. VICTORY

When someone's allegiance is not to a rule book but to a divine-human Person, how he longs to hear of all that Person's achievements—and how encouraging it is to be reminded that we are to share in his eternal victory over sin and death.

I Cor.

15:17   If you have not been raised *from the dead*
          my faith is futile
          and I am still in my sins ...
19   I am of all men most to be pitied.

20   But in fact
          you have been raised from the dead ...
21   As by *the first* man came death,
          by *this second* Man
          has come the resurrection of the dead.
22   For as in Adam all died,
          so all in you, O Christ,
          shall all be made alive ...
23   all those who belong to you ...

25   You must reign until
          you have put all enemies under your feet.
26   The last enemy to be destroyed
          is death.
          Then finally, at the end of time,
28   when all things are subjected to you,

you yourself will also be subjected
to your heavenly Father . . .
that he may be everything to every one.

41.   WHAT IS SOWN IN WEAKNESS

To affirm our Christian faith is to exult in our promised transformation in the next world. The seed of grace, "sown in weakness," is already germinating in our hearts; we have only to wait and it will
rise "in power." We pray that we be enabled to focus our wandering
eyes more steadily on these encouraging vistas of truth.

I Cor.

It is a difficulty, not a doubt, Lord,
but I do ask myself
15:35   "How are the dead raised?
With what kind of a body do they come?"

36   *I know well enough that* what I sow
does not come to life unless it dies.

37   And what I sow
is not the body which is to be,

38   but a bare kernel . . . and your Father
gives it a body as he has chosen,
and to each kind of seed its own body . . .

40   There are celestial . . . and terrestrial bodies;
but the glory of the celestial is one,

and the glory of the terrestrial is another.

41 There is one glory of the sun,
and another glory of the moon,
and another glory of the stars;
for star differs from star in glory.

42 So it is, *you have assured me,*
with the resurrection of the dead.
What is sown is perishable,
what is raised is imperishable.

43 It is sown in dishonor,
it is raised in glory.
It is sown in weakness, it is raised in power.

44 It is sown a physical body,
it is raised a spiritual body . . .

47 The first man, *Adam,* was from the earth,
a man of dust;
the second man, *you, my Lord and Savior,*
are from heaven.

49 *And I firmly believe that* as we
have born the image of the man of dust,
we shall also bear your image—
the image of the man of heaven.

42. THE WORLD TO COME

What is it that has deceived us about death? How can so many Christians experience unmitigated terror at its approach? How diametrically different was Paul's understanding. True, elsewhere he speaks about the sorrows of departure; but what are these in comparison with the incorruptible life that will clothe our mortal nature?

I Cor.

15:51   *I rejoice and wonder at your* mystery:
        We shall not all sleep,
        but we shall all be changed,
52   in a moment,
        in the twinkling of an eye,
        at the last trumpet.
        For the trumpet will sound,
        and the dead will be raised imperishable,
        and we shall be changed.

53   For this perishable nature
        must put on the imperishable,
        and this mortal nature
        must put on *your gift of* immortality.
54   When the perishable puts on the imperishable,
        and the mortal puts on immortality,
        then shall come to pass
        your saying *in scripture:*
        "Death is swallowed up in victory."

55   O death, where is thy victory?
        O death, where is thy sting? ...
57   Thanks be to our Father in heaven
        who gives us the victory
        through you, Lord Jesus Christ.

58   *Lord, help us* be steadfast,
        immovable,
        always abounding in your work,
        knowing that in you, O Lord,
        our labor is not in vain.

III. Prayers
from *Second Corinthians*

IF THE PRAYERS in this chapter seem at times to jump from one subject to another, it is because the Apostle's original train of thought is less connected in this letter than in others—so much so, that scholars are still debating whether it is one single letter or a collection of several, each written at a different time and for a different purpose.

Most probably it is really only one composition, an impassioned defense of his apostolate, written to counteract calumnies that were circulating against Paul in Corinth. The intense feeling of its disconnected parts—apparently dictated at different times and under changing moods—reveals the mind and heart of the Apostle as does no other letter.

In spite of its emotionally-charged disorganization, three main sections can be clearly isolated: (1) Paul's justification of his apostolic ministry; (2) the collection to be taken up for the Church of Jerusalem; (3) the Apostle's personal "boast" of all that the Lord has given him.

In the opening section of "Prayers from *Second Corinthians*" we are given the profile of a successful apostle. First comes a reaffirmation of the basic orientation of the apostolate: It is *for others* (Prayers #43, 44).

This is followed by a series of reflections on the qualities

that characterize a true apostle (Prayers #45-51): Fidelity to
Christ and his word (Prayer #45); dependence on, and confidence in, divine not human powers (Prayer #46); and, cen-
tral to this section, the acceptance of suffering, or willingness to
share in Christ's redemptive cross (Prayers #47-49). If he is
to be fully effective, a modern-day apostle must see the cross as
did St. Paul and our Lord himself, not as a permanent state of
tragic failure, but as a momentary, painful step towards victory
and eternity (Prayers #50, 51).

The second section of the letter is a fund-raising appeal,
and one that goes to the very root of our solidarity in Christ
and of our consequent responsibility for his world-wide plan of
salvation. The Apostle gives us two frank, clear-sighted medita-
tions on the use of money and on the responsibility of Christians who have it (Prayers #52, 53).

Finally Paul's "boast" should provide our insecure generation with much needed certitude and encouragement, for we,
too, are the object of God's special love. And we, too, can (and
must) count on his all-powerful encouragement and support
(Prayers #54-58), making our own the Apostle's confident as-
sertion: "When I am weak, then I am strong."

43. BEYOND MY STRENGTH

For Paul a painful obstacle—even a mortal trial that tempts him to
"despair of life itself"—is never a purely negative thing. Always it is
an event of positive, supernatural value, *a cross rather than a frustration*. When Christ prayed in the Garden of Olives, an angel came

"to encourage" or "to strengthen" him (the root meaning of the Latin, *con-fortare,* which has been so unhappily softened by translators into the English word, "comfort"). So strengthened, he died for us and in rising from the dead opened the way for us to rise with him from "death" to life. Now, therefore, we too pray for strength to bear the cross—not for ourselves alone, but also "for the salvation of others."

II Cor.

1:3   Father of mercies
           and God of all *strength,*

4   who *strengthens* us
           in all our affliction,
           so that we may be able to *strengthen*
           those who are in any affliction ...

5   Those who share abundantly
           in your sufferings, O Christ,
           through you *are able* to share abundantly
           in *strength* too.

6   If I am afflicted,
           it is for ... the salvation of others;
           and if I am *encouraged,* it is for their *encourage-
              ment* ...
           If others must share in my sufferings,
           bring them also, Lord, to share in my *source of
              strength* ...

          There may be times in life when
8   I am so utterly, unbearably crushed

that I despair of life itself ...

9   but this is to make me rely
not on myself, but on you, my God.

44. SHARING IN CHRIST

The strength we have just prayed for comes from the Father. It is
ours for the asking—if we ask it not for ourselves alone but also
for others, and if we are resolved to make effective use of the help
he gives us, sharing it with others who are so desperately in need.

II Cor.

1:12   *May I learn* to behave in the world
with holiness and sincerity,
not by earthly wisdom
but by your grace, O God.

*And if I have shared with my brothers
your grace and your strength,*
14   they will be proud of me,
as I will be of them,
on the day of the Lord, Jesus ...

21   Father in heaven,
it is you who have established us with you
in Christ.
You have commissioned us,

22   and put your seal upon us,
          and given us your Spirit in our hearts
          as a guarantee.

45.   PEDDLERS OF THE GOSPEL?

There was a time when I spoke of "my duty" or "my task" of witnessing to Christ in the modern world. How could I have thought
of this as anything other than a supreme privilege?

II Cor.

          Help us, Lord, to give
2:14   thanks to your Father,
          who ... always leads us in triumph,
          and through us spreads the fragrance
          of his truth and his love.
15   For we are your aroma, O Christ,
          to the Father,
          among those who are being saved ...

16   Who is sufficient for *this high calling?*
          Grant that we may not become
17   mere peddlers of your divine word.
          Help us rather to be men of sincerity
          commissioned by your Father,
          when in his sight,
          we speak of you, O Christ.

46. THE SPIRIT WRITES

Paul's own mind in this prayer is by no means clear. But we can hope, each of us, to understand, and make our own, at least one of the colors that flashes from the prism of his words: If we accept the daily events in life as opportunities to bring Christ and his encouragement to our companions, then we can count on his Spirit transforming not only our neighbor but also ourselves.

II Cor.

> *Too long have I been content, Lord,*
> *to leave your word frozen in books.*

13:2   Now I myself *am commissioned to be*
your letter of recommendation . . .
to be known
and read by all men.

3   I am to be a letter from you, O Christ . . .
written not with ink
but with the Spirit of the living God,
not on tablets of stone,
but on the tablet of my human heart . . .

5   Not that I am sufficient of myself
to claim anything as coming from me.
My sufficiency is from your Father,

6   who has qualified me
to be a minister of his new covenant,
not in a written code but in the Spirit . . .

17   And where your Spirit is,
there is freedom.

18   And we ... beholding your glory, O Lord,
            and being changed into your likeness
            from one degree of glory to another.

47.   LIGHT IN DARKNESS

If I am receptive, then Christ's light will shine from my life to
illumine mankind. Even *my* life, therefore, can be significant—and
to a high degree. But the measure of its significance may well be determined by the amount of Christ's cross that I am asked to shoulder. I pray for the insight to understand apparent failure, and for
the wisdom to accept it as Christ did—as a preliminary step, leading
to lasting, eternal victory.

II Cor.

            When you created the world, Eternal Father,
4:6   you said: "Let light shine out of darkness."
            Now you have shone in our hearts
            to give
            the light of the knowledge of your glory ...

7   But we have this treasure
            in earthen vessels
            to show that the transcendent power
            belongs to you, O God,
            and not to us.

            But all this power and knowledge is inside us.
8   *Outside* we are afflicted in every way,

but not crushed;
perplexed, but not driven to despair;
9   persecuted, but not forsaken;
struck down, but not destroyed;
10   always carrying in our bodies
the death of your Son, Jesus Christ,
so that his life
may also be manifested in our bodies.

11   While we live
we are always being given up to death
for Jesus' sake,
so that the life of Jesus
may be manifested in our mortal flesh.

48.   WHAT IS UNSEEN

The mountaineer does not spend his breath complaining about the hardness of the rock. No, the harder the rock, the surer his grip and the more certain the goal. Always his mind is concentrated on the ultimate peak which—though unseen—he knows to be beyond the next ridge. In contrast, why am I so spiritually nearsighted? What is it that keeps me from steadfastly fixing my mind and my heart on the sunlit mountains of God?

II Cor.

> *Father in Heaven,*
> *in union with Christ on the cross,*
> *we dedicate our labor, suffering, and tears*
> *to the life of these our brothers whom you love.*

4:12   So when death is at work in us,
           may it be a source of life in them ...

14   I know, *and trust,*
           that you who raised my Lord Jesus
           will raise me also with him,
           and bring me into your presence ...

16   So I do not lose heart.
           Though my outer nature is wasting away,
           my inner nature
           is being renewed every day.
17   For this slight, momentary affliction
           is preparing for me
           an eternal weight of glory
           beyond all comparison.

18   *Help us, Lord,* to look
           not to the things that are seen
           but to the things that are unseen;
           for the things that are seen
           are transient,
           but the things that are unseen
           are eternal.

49.   EXILES

The chosen home of man's immortal soul is man's glorified body;
and the body's only true and lasting home is heaven. In Neo-
Platonic thought, the body was a prison from which the soul longed

to escape. Not so in Christian thought. My body is not a prison; it
is a masterpiece of God's creation, and it will be given back to me
transformed, at the end of the world. Meanwhile, anxious though I
am to be with Christ and the saints, with my body glorified and immortal, I will still be "of good courage," as I await that ultimate day.

II Cor.

5:1   *At times we forget, but* we know, Lord,
            that if this earthly tent we live in
            is destroyed,
            we will have a building from your **Father**,
            a resurrected and glorified body,
            a house not made with hands,
            eternal in the heavens.

2   Here indeed we groan,
            and long to put on our heavenly dwelling...

4   For while we are still in this tent,
            we sigh with anxiety...
            We would be further clothed,
            so that what is mortal
            may be swallowed up by life.

5   It is your Father who has prepared us...
            and has given us his Spirit
            as a guarantee;
            grant us to be always of good courage.

6   We know
            that while we are at home in the body
            we are away from you, O Lord.

7   But we walk by faith, not by sight,
8   *hence our prayer to be* of good courage,
        even though we would rather
        be away from this *mortal* body
        and at home with you.

50.   SEEING CHRIST

I am told, and I pay lip service to the fact, that the Christian "is a
new creation"—that in some real but mysterious way he carries
within himself a new life, Christ's life. But how far I am from really
accepting in heart and *action* the fact that every day I pass Christ in
the street, ride with him on the bus, and serve him at the shop or
in the office—and that I am charged with the privileged task of
ministering to his growth in the souls of my brethren.

II Cor.

5:14   May your love, O Christ,
          be the power that controls us . . .
15   You died for us all,
          that those who live
          might live no longer for themselves
          but for you, who for our sake
          died and was raised.

16   From now on, therefore, *I am resolved*
          to regard no one from a human point of view
          as a mere natural being . . .

17   For if any one is in you, O Christ,
          he is a new creation;
          the old has passed away and the new has come.

18   All this, *of course, is a gift*
          from your Heavenly Father,
          who through you reconciled us to himself
          and gave us *in turn the privilege*
          of bringing to others this reconciliation.

19   Your Father was in you,
          reconciling the world to himself,
          not counting our trespasses against us.
          Now he has entrusted to us his message . . .

20   *Help us to live in such a way*
          that we may be your ambassadors, O Christ,
          with your Father making his appeal
          through us.

51.   LIFE OF AN APOSTLE

Had Christ been only a Hebrew prophet, a Roman orator, or a
Greek god, he might have expected immediate "success" with his
inspired teaching and miracles. But then the Twelve would have
expected immediate success also. And I, too, would have been just as
demanding, asking for equal treatment. Indeed I may still get equal
treatment—equal to what my Lord *actually* received. O, may he so

fill my mind and heart with his grace, that I will be fully willing to shoulder—with him—the inescapable crosses of a Christian's life.

II Cor.

6:1   *I pray that I may* not accept your grace
         in vain.
         As your representative, I want to
3   put no obstacle in any one's way,
         so that no fault may be found
         with my ministry *or with your Church.*

4   As your servants, O God,
         we *ask for the strength to* commend ourselves ...
         through great endurance,
         in afflictions, hardships, calamities ...
         labors, watching, and hunger.

6   *Teach us* purity and knowledge,
         forbearance, kindness ... and genuine love.
7   *And help us really to trust*
         in the power of your heavenly Father,
         fighting with the weapons of righteousness
         for the right hand and for the left,
8   in honor and dishonor,
         in ill repute and good repute.

         For your sake
         we are ready to be treated as imposters,
         though in fact we are true;
9   as unknown, and yet well known;

as dying, and behold we live;
as punished, and yet not killed;
10   as sorrowful, yet always rejoicing;
as poor, yet making many rich;
as having nothing,
and yet possessing everything.

52. MONEY

Next on the agenda in Paul's mind is his collection for the Christians in Jerusalem. The Corinthians have already pledged their assistance. But *why* are they giving? It is so easy to lose sight of one's true motivation. If my own motives were more sincere and more clearly in mind, my gift—both of money and of self—would, I am sure, be less unworthy of Christ and of his cause.

II Cor.

                There have always been fervent Christians
8:2   who in their abundance of joy,
in spite of extreme poverty,
have overflowed in a wealth of liberality . . .
3   They gave according to their means,
and beyond their means,
of their own free will, begging earnestly
4   for the favor
of taking part in the relief of *their fellows.*

I am comparing myself
8   *with* the earnestness of others
       to test if my love also is genuine.

       I should not need to be reminded
9   of you, my Lord Jesus Christ,
       that though you were rich,
       yet for our sake you became poor,
       so that by your poverty
       we might become rich.

53.   MONEY AGAIN

Contributing to the Church in Jerusalem—and to the Church right
here in my own country—must not be a painful effort but a cheerful
response, the spontaneous gift of one loving brother to another who
is in need. Were my spiritual vision only a little clearer, I would
perhaps be able to give of my time, effort, and money in this truly
Christian spirit.

II Cor.

       O God, I know that what you ask of me
9:5   is not an exaction
       but a willing gift.
       And you have reminded me that
6   he who sows sparingly
       will also reap sparingly,
       but he who sows bountifully

will also reap bountifully.

7   *Help me, then, to give* not reluctantly
or under compulsion,
for you love a cheerful giver.

8   You are able to provide me
with every blessing in abundance,
so that I may always have enough ...
for every good work ...

10   You who supply seed to the sower
and bread for food
will supply and multiply my resources
and increase my harvest ...

13   May I glorify you, O God,
by my obedience in acknowledging your gospel,
and by the generosity of my contribution
for *my fellow Christians* and for all others ...

14   Thanks be to you, my God,
for your inexpressible gift!

54. THE CURSE OF INSECURITY

We are told to "see Christ"—to recognize his authority—in religious superiors. Surprisingly this is frequently easier for the subject to do than it is for the superior. When I am given authority—whether as a general or sergeant in the army of Christ—I must learn to recog-

nize in whose name and with whose power I speak. Then perhaps I
will be less insecure, less on the defensive, less autocratic—more confident in him who strengthens me and, therefore, more able to act
with the courtesy and "gentleness of Christ."

II Cor.

When I act in your cause, Almighty God,
help me to speak with the courtesy

10:1   and gentleness of Christ.

2   *At the same time I ask for* confidence
        to show against any who suspect me
        of acting in worldly fashion.

3   Though I live in the world
        I am not carrying on a worldly war:

4   for the weapons of my warfare
        are not worldly and they have
        divine power to destroy strongholds.

        I trust that you will enable me

5   to destroy arguments
        and every proud obstacle
        to the knowledge of you, my God.
        May I take every thought captive
        and put it in the service of Christ.
        But help me keep in mind the fact that

8   the authority which you give me, Lord,
        is for building people up
        and not destroying them.

True I can and should boast of all
you have given me—but only if you
impress on my mind your saying in scripture,
17   "Let him who boasts, boast of the Lord."
        For it is not the man who commends himself
        that is accepted,
        but the man whom you commend.

55. SO WILLING TO BE DECEIVED!

How complicated is the world, and how easy it is to slide away from the true spirit of Christ. I have pledged him my troth, yes. But I have the mind of a gnat and the affections of a butterfly. Still he knows this and continues to love me. But what can I do on my part to be faithful to his love? I can ask his help; that's what I can do!

II Cor.

11:2   I am betrothed to you, O Christ,
        to be presented as a pure bride
        to her one husband.

3   But I am afraid
        that as the serpent deceived Eve by his cunning
        my thoughts may be led astray
        from a sincere and pure devotion to you.

4   *I know that sooner or later* someone will come
        and preach *another plan of salvation,*
        a "more enlightened way of life," another Jesus

than you *whom I have known;*
and I am afraid that I may accept
a different gospel
from the one I have accepted.

13 *You have warned me of* false apostles,
deceitful workmen,
disguising themselves as your apostles.

14 And no wonder, for *you have taught me*
that even Satan disguises himself
as an angel of light.
I am so easily deceived!
I will trust, therefore, not in my own
dim vision and uncertain feelings,
but in you, my only Lord and God.

56. COMPLAINING?

It was the mysterious ways of God's love that occasioned Teresa of Avila's playful complaint: "If this is how you treat your friends, Lord, no wonder you have so few of them!" Although by her standards I may not be one of his intimates, I do really want to be one of them. Would that I could see more of *his* love and less of *my* frustration in the constant daily trials of my life.

II Cor.

When I open my mouth to complain, Lord,
help me to remember how your really close friends

11:23   *have fared*—with far greater labors,
           far more imprisonments,
           with countless beatings,
           and often near death . . .

25   They have been shipwrecked . . .
           and adrift at sea.
26   *They have been* on frequent journeys,
           in danger from rivers,
           in danger from robbers,
           in danger from their own people,
           and in danger from *strangers.*

           With your help, they have not recoiled
           from danger in the city,
           danger in the wilderness,
           danger at sea,
           danger from false brethren.
27   *They have lived* in toil and hardship,
           through many a sleepless night,
           in hunger and thirst,
           often without food,
           in cold and exposure.
           These, Lord, have been your special friends.
           Why, then, am I so reluctant
           to share the weight of your cross?

57.   WEAKNESS AND STRENGTH

Faulty vision, mistaken facts, error of judgment—each of these human failings is "a thorn in my flesh." I am weak and humiliated: so weak that I am unable to walk in the paths of truth, and I must ask God to pick me up and carry me along. Then see with what determined strides he will step across the world—with me still in his arms. "For when I am weak, then I am strong."

II Cor.

12:7   To keep me from being too elated
         by the abundance *of your blessings,*
         you have given me a thorn in the flesh
         And often, as you know so well,

8   I besought you about this
         that it should leave me.

9   But you said to me:
         "My grace is sufficient for you,
         for my power
         is made perfect in weakness."

         Help me, then, all the more gladly
         to boast of my weaknesses,
         that your power, O Christ,
         may rest upon me.

10   *Teach me to be* content
         with weaknesses,

insults, hardships,
persecutions and calamities;

For when I am weak,
then I am strong.

58.   THE MEASURE OF OUR STRENGTH

Has the Church failed? Is this really Christ's work, this thing that
dies so helplessly beneath the nailed boots of dictatorship; that suf-
focates under the confiscatory taxes of so-called democracies; that is
so often enfeebled by the general apathy and weakness of its own
members? Yes, our Lord himself chose to be weak on the cross as
part of a plan to show forth, in the Resurrection, the all-encompas-
sing strength of his divinity. May this power of the Resurrection
begin now to transform not only the great history of the Church,
but also the little events of my own Christian life.

II Cor.

13:3   *Must we have* proof
that Christ is speaking in *the Church?*

He is not weak in dealing with us,
but he is powerful in us.
4   He was crucified in weakness,
but now he lives by your power, Eternal Father.
And we are weak in him,

but ... we shall also live with him
by your power, O God.

5   *Help us to* examine ourselves,
to see whether we are holding to the faith:
Do we realize
that Jesus Christ is in us? . . .

7   We pray, Eternal Father,
that we may not do wrong.
Teach us to do what is right,
though we may seem to have failed.

11   *Help us to* agree with one another,
to live in peace,
so that you, O God of love and peace,
may be with us.

14   May the grace of our Lord Jesus Christ,
and your love, Eternal Father,
and the fellowship of your Holy Spirit
be with us all.

IV. Prayers from *Galatians*

Galatians WAS WRITTEN under the stress of shock and vivid emotion. Was it possible that the new Christian communities in Asia Minor, so recently full of fervor, were already in danger of abandoning Christ? So-called Judaizers were disturbing them with talk about the divine institution of the Old Law—and here was Paul proclaiming that Christ had fulfilled and abrogated the Law.

Who was this Paul? they asked. And by whose authority did he preach such blasphemy? Why, he himself had never even seen Jesus!

The Apostle's reply—a justification both of his personal authority and of his doctrine—seethes with indignation against the false teachers. He is angrily disappointed by the fickleness of his new converts. But somehow the anger does not appear in the selections of this chapter. Perhaps because only those passages could be selected for transposition that were already prayerful, already more calm and reflective.

The prayers in this chapter center around those basic virtues Paul would like to see rekindled among the Galatians—love of God and love of neighbor rather than mere external religious observances (Prayer #64), spiritual renewal (Prayer #61), sensitivity to the differing movements of nature and grace (Prayer #65), and a wholesome, intelligent acceptance of Christ's cross (Prayer #67).

Always, of course, there is an emphasis on "life in Christ" and on the "indwelling of the Holy Spirit" (Prayer #60). It is this that renders basically unchristian any discrimination because of race, color, or creed (Prayer #62). And it is this presence in the Christian of a divine, dynamic force that should drive him ever "forward and upward" (Prayer #63).

59. UNKNOWN TO FAME

Cooperation, forbearance, and human kindness are indeed basic Christian virtues—but they can be corrupted into mere business expedients or social conventions. Have I accepted too uncritically our modern cult of public relations? Am I so concerned about what others think that I forget about what Christ thinks?

Gal.

1:1   *My life's vocation* is not from men
        nor through man,
        but through you, my Lord Jesus Christ,
        and through God your Father
        who raised you from the dead.

        My deepest allegiance must be to you
4   who gave yourself for our sins
        to deliver us
        from the present evil age,
        according to the will of your Father;
5   to whom be glory for ever and ever . . .

10   Am I now seeking the favor of men
    or of God, our Father?
    Am I trying to please men?
    If I were still pleasing men,
    I should not be your servant, O Christ.
    Teach me, then, to be less concerned
    about what others say about me,
    and ever more concerned about what you say.

60. HIDDEN SPLENDOR

Existence today is so tragically devoid of the spiritual, so replete with psychological boredom. Everywhere we see the loneliness of man and the emptiness of life. Is there anyone to bear witness to the divine, to the presence of a God who is closer to us than we are to ourselves? Who will lead my neighbor to a living contact with Christ? Can I? Is it pride on my part to think that it is up to me to do so? Or is this only the humble recognition that what he has given me is not mine to hoard? If I have received Christ I must not hide him. I am to be the visibility of his love and of his person. For only one contact with him—if it be a real personal encounter—is enough to burn away the soul-sickness of any man in this world of ours.

Gal.

    The Good News I have received
1:11   is not man's gospel.
12   For I did not receive it *just* from man . . .
    It came through a revelation

from you, O Christ, *guarded for me*
in your Church through the centuries.

15   Your Father set me apart
         before I was born,
         and called me through his grace.
16   He was pleased to reveal his Son to me,
         in order that I might *witness to you*
         among the nations.

         Give me, I pray, wisdom and resolve
2:19   that I might live to God.
20   I have been crucified with you, O Christ;
         may it be no longer I who live,
         but you who live in me.

         The life I now live in the flesh,
         may I live it by faith in the Son of God—
         in you who loved me
         and gave yourself for me.

61.   BROKEN RESOLVE

As a child I went to Sunday School, studied religion in class, and prayed often in church. I started out well enough. But then the multicolored lights of the city dazzled me, and its insistent clamor drowned out the voice of God. Is it too late now to begin again?

Gal.

3:1   O foolish *idiot that I am!*
         Who has bewitched me—
         me, before whose eyes you, my Jesus,
         were publicly portrayed as crucified? . . .

3   Am I so foolish?
         Having begun with the Spirit,
         am I now ending with the flesh?
4   Did I experience so many things in vain?

         Lord, I will never believe
         that it really was in vain.
         No, it is never too late to begin again.
         I know that it is never too late
         for the prodigal to return home.

62.   DISCRIMINATING DISCRIMINATION

How do I know if I am really united with Christ? How can I measure my love of God? My Christian neighbor is more Christ than colored, more Christ than Semite, more Christ than poor. Do I love my Lord, therefore, when I meet him in the streets? That is the question; that is the test.

Gal.

3:26   In you, O Christ,
         we are all sons of the Father

through faith.

27   For as many of us
        as were baptized into you
        have put on *your person,* O Christ.

28   There is neither Jew nor Greek,
        neither white nor colored,
        neither slave nor free,
        neither rich nor poor,
        there is neither male nor female;
        for we are all one in you, Lord.
29   And if we are yours,
        then we are . . . heirs according to promise.
        And we look forward to the day of eternity
        when we will be with you, and with all
        who have been given to share in your life.

63.   FORWARD AND UPWARD

A major theme in the best of contemporary spiritual writing is the
forward-sweeping evolution of God's plan for mankind. At long
last we have rediscovered a key concept of Pauline Christianity. In-
heritors of a hundred thousand years of God's patient, careful preparation of the world for Christianity, we are now asked to devote our
waking energies to its fuller spiritual evolution. May I learn to be
less attached to the undemanding, static present, and more coura-
geously ready to participate in the forward movement of Christ's

Gal.

    For over a hundred thousand years
4:1   *man was like* an heir,
    who as long as he is a child
    is no better than a slave . . .
2   and is under guardians and trustees
    until the date set by his father . . .
3   So with us, *members of the human race,*
    when we were children,
    we were slaves to the elemental spirits
    of the universe.

4   But when the time had fully come,
    the Father sent forth his Son,
    you, my Lord, Jesus Christ,
    born of woman,
    born under the law
5   to redeem those who were under the law,
    so that we might receive adoption
    as sons . . .

6   He has sent the Spirit of his Son,
    your Spirit, O Lord,
    into our hearts,
    crying, "Abba! Father!"
7   So through your Father
    I am no longer a slave but a son,
    and if a son then an heir.

8   Formerly, *in prehistoric times,*
    when we did not know God,

we were in bondage
to beings that by nature are not gods;
9   but now that I have come to know God,
or rather to be known by him,
how can I turn back again
to the weak and beggarly elemental spirits,
whose slaves I want to be once more?
And yet I am still tempted to worship
at the shrine of Power,
or burn incense to Venus,
10   *or superstitiously* observe days
and months and seasons and years!

Instead of going backwards in time
and downward,
may I now go forward and upward
into the new world that is being formed—
confident that you, Lord,
11   have not labored over me in vain.

64.   LOVE OR REGULATIONS

The Galatians were in real spiritual danger. Judaizers were insisting on the absolute necessity of external, legalistic practices. St. Paul,
therefore, wrote to define the power and limits of Christian liberty,
and he wrote to persons expert in misunderstanding him. Again
today the true notion of Christian liberty is threatened by a legal-

istic, overly rule-conscious mentality. For some, therefore, this
prayer of St. Paul may be of special relevance.

Gal.

5:1   You, Lord, have set me free.
           Help me to stand fast, therefore,
           and not submit again to a yoke of slavery.
           If I concentrate only on rules and regulations,
2   you, O Christ, will be of no advantage to me.
4   *If I plan on* being justified by the law
           and by external observances,
           I have fallen away from grace.
5   For it is through your Spirit,
           by faith, *that I am to be saved—*
6   by faith working through love.

7   *Till some time ago* I was running well;
           what hindered me from obeying the truth?
           Is my religion becoming just
           a series of routine, external practices?

13   We were called to freedom.
           Teach us, Lord, not to use our freedom
           as an opportunity for *selfishness,*
           but through love to be servants of one another,
14   *remembering that* the whole law
           is fulfilled in one word:
           "You shall love your neighbor as yourself."

65.   NATURE OR SPIRIT

The flesh and the spirit, the old man and the new, nature and grace
—these keys to the mind of St. Paul were fashioned both by revelation and by personal experience. His conversion on the road to
Damascus was but the first of many reminders of his own human
weakness, and of God's overriding strength and goodness. In Paul's
view the Christian life is a life "in Christ," a life of increasing openness to motions from above, of growing sensitivity to the impulses
of the Spirit. But the aim of this Divine Spirit from above—as we
saw at greater length in the introduction to Prayer #8—is not to
draw us away from the material world, but rather to deepen our
commitment to it by increasing the selflessness and purity of our
intention.

Gal.

5:16   *May I learn* to walk by the Spirit,
           and not gratify the desires of the flesh.

17   For the desires of the flesh
           are against the Spirit,
           and the desires of the Spirit
           are against the flesh.
           How well I know, Lord, that
           these are opposed to each other,
           and prevent me from doing what I would . . .

19   The works of the flesh are plain:
           immorality, impurity . . .
           enmity, strife, jealousy, anger, selfishness . . .
           drunkenness, carousing, and the like.

And you have warned me . . .
that those who do such things
shall not inherit your kingdom.

22   But the fruit of the Spirit, *you assure me,*
is love, joy, peace,
patience, kindness, goodness,

23   faithfulness, gentleness, and self-control . . .

24   Those who belong to you, Christ Jesus,
have crucified the flesh with its passions.

25   *Help us now* to live by the Spirit . . .
and walk by the Spirit.

66.   USELESS COMPARISONS

There is no law of relativity in spiritual things. At least there is no legitimate way of measuring myself against my neighbor's achievements. For one has been given ten talents, another five, and another but one. And only he who gave them knows what return is possible. Meanwhile I am not to delude myself into thinking that I personally coined the talents. No, all that I am and all that I have is an exciting gift to be enjoyed—and to be used with hard-working but tension-free perseverance.

Gal.

5:26   *Teach us, Lord,* to have no self-conceit,
no provoking of one another,
no envy of one another.

6:1   If a man is *found guilty of* any trespass,
       you want us to be spiritual
       and to restore him in a spirit of gentleness.
       Teach us to look to ourselves,
       lest we too be tempted.

2   *And help us* to bear one another's burdens,
       and so fulfil your law, O Christ.

       Impress upon me, Lord, the fact that
3   if I think I am something,
       when I am nothing,
       I am deceiving myself.
       And above all, keep me from boasting that I am
       doing more than someone else!

4   Let me test my own work,
       and then my reason to boast
       will be in myself alone and not in my neighbor.
5   For each of us has to bear his own load
       not his neighbor's. And only you, Lord, can say
       just what it is you want me to carry.

67. A PERISHABLE HARVEST?

Nowhere are the contrasting motions of "nature" and of "spirit" so
evident as in our hunger for thanks and our longing for fame.
Christ's cross is a salutary counter argument. But it is not—as some
neurotically imagine—a symbol that failure is the Christian ideal.

Christ did not fail: From the cross he founded his world-wide Church. The cross was valuable not in itself but as the means of achieving a higher goal. It was but a stage in our conquest of sin, suffering, and death. As such it is a symbol not of despair but of hope—a source of resolution, determination, and courage in our collective quest of eternal life.

Gal.

6:7 *You have told me that* whatever a man sows,
   that he will also reap;

8 that he who sows to his own *selfish ambitions*
   will from the flesh reap corruption;
   but he who sows to the Spirit
   will from the Spirit reap eternal life.

9 Do not let me grow weary, then,
   in well-doing,
   for in due season I shall reap,
   if I do not lose heart.

10 *Meanwhile, help me when* I have the opportunity,
   to do good to all men,
   and especially to those
   who are of the household of faith.

  There are times when I am tempted
12 to make a good showing . . .
   in order that I may not be persecuted
   for your cross . . .

14 But far be it from me to glory
   except in your cross,

O Lord Jesus Christ,
by which the world has been crucified to me,
and I to the world.

And I pray for the realization that
17   no man can trouble me,
if I bear on my body the marks of *your suffering.*
For then your grace, O Lord Jesus Christ,
will be with my spirit. Amen.

V. Prayers from *Ephesians*

"WE ARE no longer strangers and sojourners, but we are fellow citizens with the saints and members of the household of God" (Prayer #71). This poignant statement of faith and hope was written from a prison cell in Rome—a setting that makes even more impressive the great hymn of praise to "the breadth and length and height and depth [of the love of God] . . . which surpasses knowledge" (Prayer #72). For it was while contemplating this eternal splendor of the Father, that Paul gave thanks for the privilege bestowed on him of "making known" to the Gentiles, even from prison, "the unsearchable riches of Christ."

Ephesians seems to have been written as a circular letter to the Christian communities of Asia Minor, for whom Paul was "an ambassador in chains . . . [speaking his mind boldly] to proclaim the mystery of the gospel" (Prayer #78).

The theme of man's helplessness and of God's eternal strength manifesting itself in Christ is a recurring subject in Ephesians (Prayers #68,69,70). Upon this is built the second section, the moral teachings of the letter: The unity in diversity that should characterize the members of Christ's body (Prayer #73); the calming of rancor and the mutual charity that should follow (Prayers #74,75); and the Christian exercise of authority both in the home and at work (Prayers #76,77). The section concludes (Prayer #78) with a restatement of the theme in warrior terms, with man's shielding his natural weakness and vulnerability by putting on the armor of Christ: "the breastplate of righteousness . . . the shield of faith . . . the helmet of salvation, and the sword of the Spirit."

68.   FULFILLMENT

Surely to be normal—to be fully sane—requires that I be more than just an "average," reflecting the "normal" doubts, confusion, and drugged hopelessness of this twentieth century. Sanity like sanctity has its only real measure, or norm, in Christ. Using the word in the best sense, therefore, I will be "normal" only to the extent that I conform to the Ultimate Norm, to the extent that I am like the only measure of humanity that really counts.

Eph.

1:3   O God,
          Father of our Lord Jesus Christ . . .

4   you have chosen us in him
          before the foundation of the world,
          that we should be holy
          and blameless before him.

5   You destined us in love
          to be your sons
          through Jesus Christ,
          according to the purpose of your will . . .

7   In him we have redemption
     through his blood,
     the forgiveness of our trespasses,
     according to the riches of your grace
8   which you lavished upon us.

9   You have made known to us
     in all wisdom and insight
     the mystery of your will,
     according to your purpose
     which you set forth in Christ.
10   Your plan for the fullness of time,
     is to unite all things in him,
     things in heaven and things on earth.

12   *I have* hoped in your Son, Jesus Christ,
     and have been destined and appointed to live
     for the praise of his glory.
13   I have heard the word of truth,
     the gospel of my salvation,
     and I have believed in him.
     And I have been sealed
     with the promised Holy Spirit
14   who is the guarantee of my inheritance.

     Until I acquire possession of it, O my God,
     help me to be worthy of this heritage
     you have put aside for me in heaven.

69. ABOVE ALL POWERS

I cannot direct myself with singleness of purpose away from the familiar comforts of this world towards the unfamiliar raptures of a higher one, unless first I have some inner understanding or foretaste of what is in store for me there. Poverty of spirit makes sense only if it introduces me to a deeper and more complete fulfillment. I pray, therefore, that "the eyes of my heart be enlightened."

Eph.

1:17   Father of glory,
        I ask and pray for
        a spirit of wisdom and of revelation . . .
18   that the eyes of my heart be enlightened,
        that I may know what is the hope
        to which you have called me,
        what are the riches
        of your glorious inheritance in the saints,
19   and what is the immeasurable greatness
        of your power in us who believe.

        May I learn to measure it by
        the working of your great might
20   which you accomplished in Christ,
        when you raised him from the dead
        and made him sit at your right hand
        in the heavenly places—
21   far above all rule and authority
        and power and dominion,

and above every name that is named,
not only in this age
but also in that which is to come.

70. ROOM FOR PRIDE

I have some idea what it is to follow the sinful "course of this world." But my distant forebearers, rescued from the pervasive paganism of their primitive cultures, knew this with a "realer" knowledge, perhaps with some of the vivid conviction that animated Saint Paul as he watched the greedy Roman crowds elbowing their way into the gladiatorial arenas. Now, at any rate, I am beholden to God for a double grace: For the religious convictions he has given through my parents and my culture, and for the individual, personal strength I have received more directly and immediately from his hand.

Eph.

2:1   You made us alive,
        when we were dead
        through the trespasses and sins
2   in which we once walked—
        following the course of this world,
        following ... the spirit that is now at work
        in the sons of disobedience.
3   Among these we all once lived
        in the passions of our flesh,
        following the desires of body and mind,
        and so we were by nature, children of wrath ...

4   But you, Eternal Father,
         who are rich in mercy,
         out of the great love with which you loved us,
5   even when we were dead through our trespasses,
         made us alive together with Christ ...
6   and raised us up with him,
         and made us sit
         with him in the heavenly places.

         Through the ages you have shown
7   the immeasurable riches of your grace
         in kindness toward us in Christ Jesus.
8   For by grace we have been saved
         through faith.

         I realize, Lord, that our faith
         is unmerited. It is not our own doing;
         it is your gift, O God—
9   *And it is ours* not because of works,
         lest we should boast *of our own achievement,*
10   *forgetting that we are altogether* your workmanship,
         created in Christ Jesus.

71. NO LONGER STRANGERS

To live "in the world . . . having no hope and without God,"
hurtling towards an unknown destiny across the dark, unmapped
sea of outer space, such is the fate of so many men and women in the

modern world. Clasped in one another's arms, whistling bravely in
the blackness of the night, they suppress for a time the nameless
terrors of existence. In contrast, I walk in the sunlight of God. But
I—more stupid, perhaps, than they—am afraid to open my eyes and
see.

Eph.

2:*12*   Help us to remember, Lord,
            that there was a time *in our own lives*
            and in those of our ancestors when we were
            separated from you,
            alienated from the commonwealth of Israel,
            strangers to the covenants of promise,
            having no hope and without God . . .

13   But now in you, Christ Jesus,
            we who once were far off
            have been brought near in your blood.

            Once we were separated by enmities
            of nation, color, and caste.
14   *But now* you are our peace;
            you have made us all one
            and have broken down the dividing walls
            of hostility . . .
15   You have created in yourself
            one new man
            in place of the *many antagonistic ones,*
            so making peace
16   and reconciling us all to your Father

in one body through the cross,
thereby bringing hostility to an end.

17   You came
and preached peace to us who were far off
and peace to those who were near.

18   *Now all of us* through you
have access in one Spirit to the Father.

19   We are no longer strangers
and sojourners,
but we are fellow citizens with the saints,
and members of the household of your Father,

20   built upon the foundation
of the apostles and prophets.

You, Christ Jesus, are the chief cornerstone.

21   In you the whole structure is joined together
and grows into a holy temple.

22   *And into this temple* we also are built,
living stones formed now into a dwelling
place of God.

72.   IN DEPTH AND WONDER

What is the mystery of Christ, "that was not made known to the
sons of men in other generations"? It is the whole gospel of Christ's
power and of Christ's love, a reality that goes beyond the divisions
of Jew and Gentile and embraces the whole created world. In this

passage the restless, fiery spirit of Paul "halts on the crest as though spellbound by the vista." Speaking in the solemn tones of a Hebrew prophet, "his awe-struck wonderment . . . sweeps us along in his train into the celestial holy of holies, before the throne of God."

Eph.

> *This plan of yours, Eternal Father,*
> *this proffered gift to all mankind*
> *of a new and higher level of existence,*

3:4   this "Mystery of Christ"

5   was not made known to the sons of men
> in other generations.
> It has now been revealed to us that
> *Jew and Gentile, rich and poor,*
> *yellow and white and red and black—*
> *we are all destined to be* fellow heirs,

6   members of the same body,
> and partakers of the promise
> in your Son . . .

7   Of his gospel I have been made a minister
> according to the gift of your divine grace
> which has been given me
> by the working of your power.

8   To me,
> though I am the very least of all the saints,
> this grace has been given,
> to preach to *all people and in all places*
> the unsearchable riches of Christ,

9   and to make all men see

what is the plan of this mystery
hidden for ages in you,
who created all things.

10 Through the church
your manifold wisdom, O God,
is now to be made known
to the principalities and powers ...

11 For your eternal purpose
has been realized in Christ Jesus our Lord,
in whom I have boldness and confidence ...

14 For this reason
I bow my knees before you,
Father of our Lord Jesus Christ,

15 from whom every family in heaven and on earth
is named.

16 According to the riches of your glory,
grant us, *we pray,*
to be strengthened with might
through your Spirit in the inner man:

17 that Christ your Son
may dwell in our hearts through faith;
and that we,
being rooted and grounded in love,

18 may have power to comprehend
with all the saints
what is the breadth and length
and height and depth ... of his love

19 which surpasses knowledge.

In short, we make bold to ask
what your Apostle asked:
that we may be filled
with all the fullness of God.

Eternal and all-loving Father
20   *whose* power is at work within us,
        you are able to do far more abundantly
        than all we ask or think.
21   To you be glory in the church
        and in Christ Jesus
        to all generations
        for ever and ever. Amen.

73.   ONENESS IN CHRIST

Turning from doctrine to application, Paul begins this the second section of his letter with an appeal for unity. How much longer will the work of Christ be frustrated by walls that time and childish jealousies have built between the members of his body, pitting individual against individual, clique against clique, and organization against organization? O, when will we begin to grow up "to mature manhood . . . so that we may no longer be children"?

Eph.

We need your help, Lord, if we are
4:1   to lead a life worthy of the calling
         to which you have called us . . .

2   with patience,
         forbearing one another in love,
3   eager to maintain the unity of the Spirit
         in the bond of peace.

4   There is one body and one Spirit,
         just as we were called to one hope.
5   *And we owe allegiance to* one Lord,
         one faith, one baptism,
6   one God and Father of us all,
         who is above all
         and through all and in all.

7   But grace was given to each of us
         unequally
         according to the measure of your gift.
11   *For it is your wish that some of us*
         should be apostles,
         some prophets, some evangelists,
         some pastors and teachers.
12   *And so we are equipped differently*
         for the work of the ministry,
         for building up your body, O Christ.

         Guide us, we pray, to mature manhood ...
14   so that we may no longer be children,
         tossed to and fro
         and carried about with every wind of doctrine,
         by the cunning of men,
         and by their craftiness in deceitful wiles.

15   Speaking the truth in love,
          may we grow up in every way
          into you who are the head,
          Jesus Christ our Lord.

74.   RESENTMENT

"I must no longer live . . . in the futility of my mind," with Walter
Mitty visions of grateful admirers bowing down before me. More
important, I must learn to curb my resentment when they don't bow
down, when I am passed over without recognition. What I want to
want is not the praise and recognition of men but that of the Lord.
I ask him to clothe me in a "new nature, created after the likeness
of God."

Eph.

4:17   I must no longer live . . .
           in the futility of my mind,
18   darkened in my understanding,
           alienated from the true life of God.
22   *Help me, Lord, to* put off my old nature
           which belongs to a former manner of life
           and is corrupt . . .
23   May I be renewed in the spirit of my mind,
24   and put on a new nature,
           created after your likeness, O God,
           in true righteousness and holiness.

25   *Teach us to* put away falsehood;
        let each of us speak the truth with his neighbor,
        for we are members one of another.

26   *Mindful of the saying,* "Be angry but do not sin,"
        may we not let the sun go down on our anger,

27   and may we give no opportunity to the devil.

28   Let the thief, *if thief there be in our midst,*
        no longer steal,
        but rather let him labor,
        doing honest work with his hands,
        so that he may be able to give to those in need.

29   Let no evil talk come out of our mouths,
        but only such
        as is good for *building up the faith*
        that it may impart grace to those who hear.

31   May all bitterness
        and wrath and anger and clamor
        and slander
        be put away from us.

32   *Give us the grace, Lord,*
        to be kind to one another and tenderhearted
        and forgiving one another
        as your Father forgave us
        in you, Jesus Christ.

75. ONCE WE WERE DARKNESS

"Once we were darkness," but now we have begun to move in the
light. But the fog is still thick, and the light of Christ is engaged in
a perilous struggle with new waves of obscurity that keep rolling in.
I have far to travel and cannot afford to take my eyes off the road. I
will go forward, "making the most of the time . . . [only if I] understand what the will of the Lord is."

Eph.

You have told us, Lord,
5:1   to be imitators of your Father in Heaven
as his beloved children.

2   *Help us, therefore, to* walk in love,
as you loved us
and gave yourself up for us,
a fragrant offering and sacrifice to the Father . . .

8   Once we were darkness,
but now we are light in the Lord.
May we learn to walk as children of light,
9   *knowing that* the fruit of light
is found in all that is good and right and true.

I know, Lord, that we must
15   look carefully how we walk,
not as unwise men but as wise,
16   making the most of the time,
because the days are evil.

17   May we not be foolish,
            but understand what is your will.
            Instead of filling our bellies
18   and getting drunk with wine . . .
            may we be filled with the Spirit of God,
19   addressing one another in . . . spiritual songs,
            singing and making melody to you, O Lord,
            with all our heart.

76. A HUSBAND'S PRAYER

St. Paul's instructions to married people were, of course, directed immediately to persons of a Semitic culture, separated from us by two thousand years of Christian evolution. But insecure male supremacists of all kinds still delight in citing passages like this from *Ephesians:* "The husband is the head of the wife as Christ is the head of the church . . . [hence] wives must also be subject in everything to their husbands." The Semitic idiom and emphasis in these words can be understood only after painstaking study. An easier and more direct way of discovering the mind of the Apostle might be to balance such statements with others in the very same passage that describe the role of the Christian husband:

Eph.

            For my dear wife, for our happiness together,
5:20   *for the children,* and for everything
            do I give thanks
            in your name, O Lord Jesus Christ,
            to your Father in Heaven.

As it is your will that
21 we be subject to one another
out of reverence for you,
so wives are to be subject to their husbands
as to you, my Lord.
Good! But this is only the first sentence.
25 *You go on to insist that I as a* husband
must love my wife
as you loved the church
and gave yourself up for her
26 that you might sanctify her.
So this too is your command, that I dedicate
my whole life to the woman I have married.

You gave yourself totally
27 that the church might be presented before you
in splendor,
without spot or wrinkle or any such thing;
that she might be holy and without blemish.
28 Even so, I as a husband
should love my wife as my own body ...

29 No man ever hates his own flesh,
but nourishes and cherishes it,
as you do the church,
30 because we are members of your body.
31 "For this reason,"
as you have revealed it,
"a man shall leave his father and mother

and be joined to his wife,
and the two shall become one."

32   This is a great mystery ...
33   And each one of us now *prays*
         for the faith and the patience
         really to cherish and love his wife
         as himself.

77.   AUTHORITY AND LOVE

As the obedience of a wife makes sense only in terms of the Christian dedication of her husband; so the obedience of children and the
service of employees becomes fully Christian only when balanced
by a spirit of selflessness on the part of parents or employers. How
delicate in the Christian world is this balance of love and authority
—and with what tragic results has it been ignored!

Eph.
 6:1   Children are to obey their parents
          in the Lord,
          for this is *what you direct, O God:*
 2   "Honor your father and mother ...
 3   that it may be well with you
          and that you may live long on earth."
          So much for our children. In turn,
 4   *we who are mothers and* fathers
          are not to provoke our children to anger,

but bring them up in the discipline
and instruction of the Lord—
discipline and instruction that
bear the hallmark of your divine love.

Again, those who serve others
6   *are to* do your will, O God, from the heart,
7   rendering service with a good will
as to the Lord and not to men,
8   knowing that whatever good any one does,
he will receive the same again from you.

9   *But we who are* masters
are to do the same
and show consideration for those who work
knowing that you,
who are both their master and ours,
are in heaven,
and that there is no partiality with you.

78.   CHRISTIAN WARFARE

If only I were less insecure, less timid and fearful! O, I put up a
good front—to the point of overcompensating at times, making life
miserable for others—but underneath I am miserable myself. I was
born into a world of motion and change; my companions are root-
less and without faith; and a prototype of the ultimate Bomb orbits

overhead. Is there then nothing for me to do? Is my personality set beyond repair? I am weak, yes, but not too weak to put on the armor of Christ.

Eph.

6:10 *May I learn to* be strong in you, O Lord,
    walking in the strength of your might.

11   *Give me your* armor, O God,
    that I may be able to stand
    against the wiles of the devil.

12   For I am not, *as you have warned me,*
    contending against flesh and blood,
    but against the principalities,
    against the powers,
    against the world rulers of this present darkness,
    and against the spiritual hosts of wickedness
    in the heavenly places.

13   Therefore *I must learn to* take
    the whole armor of God,
    that I may be able to withstand
    in the evil day,
    and having done all, to stand.
    I ask to serve you from now on

14   having girded my loins with truth,
    and having put on the breastplate
    of righteousness,

15   and having shod my feet
    with the equipment of the gospel of peace.

16 *With all this I will* take the shield of faith,
with which to quench all the flaming darts
of the evil one.

17 And I will take the helmet of salvation,
and the sword of the Spirit,
which is your word, O God.

18 *Teach me to* pray at all times in the Spirit,
with all prayer and supplication—
that I may keep alert
with all perseverance ...

19 to proclaim the mystery of the gospel

20 for which I am your ambassador,
that I may declare it boldly, as I ought.

VI. Prayers from *Philippians*

THE PROLOGUE of *Philippians* is joy, and joy is the theme of its epilogue. In the first chapter (Prayer #79), the Apostle sends his thoughts speeding from the gloomy surroundings of his prison cell to the encouraging growth of his work among the Christians at Philippi, the ancient birthplace of Alexander of Macedon. Then in the last chapter (Prayer #85), as a final admonition, he writes: "Rejoice in the Lord always; again I will say, Rejoice." In this chapter, his joy and his longing break out in that Aramaic formula familiar to the Christians of the early Church, *Maranatha,* "Come, O Lord."

This warm theme permeates the in-between sections of the letter as well. First comes his account (Prayers #80 & 81) of the apostolic *value* of suffering, a value that overshadows and submerges the pain and frustration of his own captivity. Next he recognizes that we live "in the midst of a crooked and perverse generation" (Prayer #82). But this he sees not as an ultimate tragedy but as a challenging opportunity for Christian service and hope, where we are to "shine as lights in the world"—a joyous affirmation of the meaning of life, clear enough and strong enough to counteract the neurotic despair so characteristic of modern man.

Finally, he would not be Paul if he did not go on to insist

that these lights must direct people towards a religion that goes beyond the externals of the Law, of contemporary rite and ritual (Prayer #83). Our task is to light up the inner meaning of existence, so that man will be able to "go forward to what lies ahead [and] press on toward the goal for the prize" (Prayer #84). And so we will attain to that "peace of God, which passes all understanding" (Prayer #85). *Maranatha!*

79.   FRIENDS IN CHRIST

Philippians is a letter to friends, to converts whose faces are warmly familiar to Paul. The good they are doing—as active apostles, not immobilized in prison like himself—bolsters up his morale, reminding him that his own life has by no means been spent in vain. So I, too, am encouraged by the fact that even the little good I have done will not die; that it continues on in the world, multiplying itself from generation to generation.

Phil.

1:3   I thank you, my God,
           in all my remembrance *of friends of yours*
           whose paths in life have crossed mine.

4   Always in every prayer of mine for them
           there is a stirring of joy.

5   I am thankful
           for their partnership in the gospel . . .

6   And I am sure
that you who began a good work in them
will bring it to completion . . .

7   I hold each of them in my heart,
for they are all partakers with me of grace,
ready for the defense
and confirmation of your gospel . . .

9   It is my prayer
that their love may abound more and more,
with knowledge
and all discernment,

10   so that they may approve what is excellent,
and may be pure and blameless
for the day of *judgment and reward.*

11   *May we all be* filled
with the fruits of righteousness
which come through you, Jesus Christ,
to the glory and praise of your Father.

80.   SUFFERING AND SUCCESS

For a person who on earth has had a foretaste of heaven—especially
if now, like Paul, he is in prison or in pain—"to live is Christ, and
to die is gain." But enjoyment of this gain may have to be postponed
if there is still much work to be done. May I be enabled to see in
my own life the great apostolic potential of frustration and suffering,

and may I learn to accept them with Christian courage and with a
non-self-centered love.

Phil.

1:12   *Lord, I take courage from the fact*
    that what has happened to me
    has really served to advance your gospel.
    For many of those who have been with me

14   have been made confident in you,
    because of my *suffering*
    and the strength you give me to accept it.
    So now they are much more bold
    to speak the word of God without fear . . .

18   You, O Christ, are proclaimed;
    and in this I rejoice.

19   Yes, and I shall rejoice.
    For I know that through my prayers
    and the help of your Spirit
    this trial will turn out for my deliverance.

20   It is my eager expectation and hope
    that I shall not be at all ashamed,
    but that with full courage now as always
    you will be honored in my body,
    whether by life or by death.

21   For to me to live is you, O Christ,
    and to die is gain.

22   *If you decide to give me* life in the flesh,
      that means fruitful labor for me.
      Yet which I shall choose I cannot tell.

23   I am hard pressed between the two.
      My desire is to depart
      and be with you, O Christ,
      for that is far better.
      But there may be some who still need me alive;

24   *if so* to remain in the flesh is more necessary
      on their account.
      Lord, the decision is yours.

25   *For my part, I am ready* to remain
      and continue with them all,
      for their progress and joy in the faith . . .

27   Only let our manner of life
      be worthy of your gospel . . .
      that we may stand firm in one spirit,
      with one mind striving side by side for the faith . . .

28   not frightened in anything by our opponents . . .

29   May it be granted to us
      that for your sake, O Christ,
      we not only believe in you
      but also suffer for you,

30   engaged in the same conflict which you saw.

81. UNTO DEATH

In the year 6 B.C., a man was born who was more than a man. His human nature was sustained in existence and made to be a person by the indwelling personality of the Eternal Word of God. In all right and justice, human nature raised to this undreamed-of excellence should have been shot through with glory, honor, and immortality. But for our sake Christ preferred to be without these divine prerogatives for a time, choosing instead to live for thirty-three long years a life of service and obscurity. It was by veiling his divine glory that he unveiled ("revealed") for all time the consuming nature of divine love. Still, the glory could not remain covered. His mission on earth accomplished, he received from his heavenly Father the Name, that is the visible authority and excellence, of the divinity.

Phil.

2:2   *May we learn to* be of the same mind,
       having the same love,

3   *Teach us to* do nothing from selfishness
       or conceit;
       but in humility
       to count others better than ourselves.

4   Let each of us
       look not only to our own interests,
       but also to the interests of others.

       In other words, Lord, give us your mind.
6   *For you,* though you were in the form of God,
       did not count equality with God

a thing to be grasped;
7   but you emptied yourself,
taking the form of a servant,
being born in the likeness of men.
8   And being found in human form
you humbled yourself
and became obedient unto death,
even death on a cross.

9   That is why your Father has highly exalted you
and bestowed on you the name
which is above every name.
And that is why in your presence
10   every knee should bow,
in heaven and on earth and under the earth,
11   and every tongue should confess
that you, Jesus Christ, are Lord,
to the glory of your Father in heaven.

82. POWER

"Work as if all depended on you; pray as if all depended on God."
Underpinning this familiar maxim is the fact that God's power is
the essential ingredient of every good work I do, as the power of the
generator is continuously present in the light bulb that shines in
my room. Now, in a "crooked and perverse generation," he wants
me to "shine as a light in the world." But I will be able to do so

only if I succeed in connecting the filament of my soul to the current of God's eternal power and love.

Phil.

                I know that it is up to me
2:12   to work out my own salvation
                with fear and trembling;
13   *but I also know that* you, my God,
                are at work in me
                both to will
                and to work.

14   *Help me to* do all things without grumbling
                or questioning,
15   that I may be blameless and innocent,
                a child of God without blemish.

                In the midst
                of a crooked and perverse generation,
                you ask us
                who have been redeemed by your Son
                to shine as lights in the world,
16   holding fast to the word of life:
                so that in the day of Christ,
                at the last judgment,
                we may be proud
                that we did not run in vain
                or labor in vain.

83. LOSS AND GAIN

Like Paul—though with measurably less conviction and intensity—
I have been a Pharisee. I have overemphasized the external practices of religion. Of course I had plenty of company: the disease is
endemic to human nature. But now I'm seriously disturbed about
it, and I want to be cured. I pray, therefore, that my eyes be opened
finally and effectively to the inner power and meaning of Christ's
death and resurrection.

Phil.

3:3   *Show me how to* worship the Father in spirit,
         to glory in you, Christ Jesus,
         and to put no confidence in *outward observances.*

5   *In the past I was* a Pharisee . . .
6   righteous under the law and blameless.
7   But whatever gain I had,
         I now count as loss
         for your sake, O Christ.
8   Indeed I count everything as loss
         because of the surpassing worth
         of knowing you, Jesus my Lord.

         For your sake I am prepared
         to suffer the loss of all things,
         and count them as refuse,
         in order that I may gain you
9   and be found in you.

10   *I pray that* I may know you
          and the power of your resurrection,
          and if it is your will, I am ready
          to share your sufferings,
          becoming like you in your death,
11   that if possible
          I may attain the resurrection from the dead.

84.   THE GOAL AND THE PRIZE

Openly and in secret The Persuaders are producing a type of man
whose "god is the belly." At least in our subconscious we are being
turned into "enemies of the cross of Christ." So many of the social
pressures in the Western world are downward. Without repeated
stimulus and powerful tugs from above, whatever momentum
upward we may have had is quickly arrested and reversed. Exter-
nally rich and comfortable; internally poverty-stricken and anxious.
How great is our need!

Phil.

          Lord, help me to get moving again
          towards the promised goal,
3:12   for I have not already obtained it,
          and I am not already perfect.
          Pull me from above, that I may
          press on to make it my own
          because you, Jesus Christ,
          have made me your own ...

13   Forgetting what lies behind
      and straining forward to what lies ahead,
14   I want to press on toward the goal
      for the prize,
      responding to the upward call of your Father
      in you, Christ Jesus.

      Preserve us, your followers,
      from the corrosive influence of so many today
18   who live as enemies of your cross, O Christ.
19   Their end, *I fear,* is destruction.
      their god is the belly,
      and they glory in their shame,
      with minds set on earthly things.
      Resisting their example,
      may we never forget
20   that our commonwealth is in heaven,
      and from it we await a Savior.

      When you come to take us home
21   *we count on you to* change our lowly body
      to be like your glorious body,
      by the power which enables you
      to subject all things to yourself.

85.   *MARANATHA*

Who is right: the exultant, joy-filled early Christians or the dour, straight-faced Puritans? And on whose side am I rooting? Do I see myself as a weighty spirit, loaded down with the self-important solemnity of the Puritans and Jansenists? Or am I still able to respond with something like the joyous spontaneity of the early Christians: *Maranatha,* "Come, O Lord!"?

Phil.

It is good to be reminded that
4:3   our names are in the book of life.
4   I rejoice in you, O Lord, always;
        again I say to myself: "Rejoice"...
5   for you, my God, are at hand.

6   May we have no anxiety,
        but in everything
        by prayer and supplication
        with thanksgiving
        let our requests be made known
        to your Father.
7   So may the peace of God,
        which passes all understanding,
        keep our hearts and our minds
        in you, Christ Jesus.

8   Finally, whatever is true,
        whatever is honorable, whatever is just,
        whatever is pure, whatever is lovely,

whatever is gracious—
if there is any excellence,
if there is anything worthy of praise—
may this be the argument of our thoughts;
9   then your Father, the God of peace,
will be with us.

10   I will rejoice in you, my Lord, . . .
11   and not complain of want . . .
In whatever state I am,
I will be content,
for you are there with me.
12   In any and all circumstances
I must learn the secret
of facing plenty and hunger,
abundance and want.

13   I can do all things in you
who strengthen me.
19   And *I firmly believe that* your divine Father
will supply every need of mine
according to his riches
in you, Christ Jesus.
30   To our God and Father be glory
for ever and ever. Amen.

VII. Prayers from *Colossians*

COLOSSAE, on the Lycus River some 110 miles inland from Ephesus, was a small wool and weaving center. Paul himself seems never to have visited it, but he was close to Epaphras who founded the Church there.

Since the community was predominantly Gentile, there was no seething problem about the Law, as there had been with the Judaizers in Galatia and elsewhere. Instead, the tensions that called forth this letter were those that came from the rise of Gnostic sects at Colossae, and the attraction they held out to the curious, half-instructed new Christians.

Paul, therefore, opens the epistle with a reminder that it is knowledge of God's will that counts, not new and esoteric revelations (Prayer #86). He then launches into an implicit but direct attack on the Gnostic cult of angelic mediators between God and man (Prayer #87). Thrones and dominions, princedoms and powers, he says, are all inferior to Christ who is the creator of all that is "visible and invisible . . . He is before all things, and in him all things hold together."

This is followed by a polemic section that reveals the Apostle's anxious concern for all "that their hearts may be encouraged . . . [and that they be] knit together in love" (Prayer #88). Next, what is really a warning against false

teachers becomes a beautiful description of the new life that we
have been given by sharing—through faith and baptism—in the
death and resurrection of Christ (Prayer #89).

Specific moral questions are solved in a final section of the
letter: children should obey their parents, slaves their masters,
wives their husbands, etc. But neither these questions nor the
Apostle's long last greetings appear in these pages. Our selection concludes, therefore, with the next-to-last chapter, where
Paul restates one of the foundations of Christian morality—the
equal and unalienable basic rights of man (Prayer #90). One
cannot help wondering what he would have said had he fore-
seen that after two thousand years of Christianity there would
still be large pockets of racial bias and discrimination; that
even among Christians there would still be "Gentile and Jew
... barbarian, Scythian, slave and free man," and that universal
Christian love would still not be accepted in practice as the
force which alone "binds everything together in perfect
harmony."

86.   INSIGHT

At Colossae, Gnostic sects boasting of private revelations seem to
have been promoting curious and esoteric religious practices. Men
and women are so easily tempted by a desire to be "on the inside,"
no matter how strange the theories that current fashion proposes.
With this in mind, Paul prays that the Christians of Colossae: "be
filled with the knowledge of [God's] will in all spiritual wisdom

and understanding." Twenty centuries later this is still my need, and
still my prayer.

Col.

1:3   I thank you my God always . . .
5   because of the hope
         laid up for us in heaven,
         and because of the gospel
6   which has come to us . . .
         and is bearing fruit and growing . . .

9   May we be filled with the knowledge of your will
         in all spiritual wisdom and understanding,
10   to lead a life worthy
         of your Son, our Lord,
         fully pleasing to him,
         bearing fruit in every good work . . .
11   May we be strengthened with all power,
         according to your glorious might,
         for all endurance
         and patience with joy.

12   We give thanks to you, our Father,
         who have qualified us to share
         in the inheritance of the saints in light.
13   For you have delivered us
         from the dominion of darkness
         and transferred us
         to the kingdom of your beloved Son.

87.   CREATOR BLESSED

Christ is the head of the Church, of course. But he is more. And
here we owe a great debt to the Gnostics, for it was their attack that
led Paul to bring us further and to show us Christ's headship of
the whole created universe. "He is the image of the invisible God
. . . in him all things were created, in heaven and on earth, visible
and invisible . . . all things were created through him and for him."
How vital, I wonder, is this realization in our spiritual life today?

Col.

          I believe, Lord, that you
1:13   *are the* beloved Son of God,
14   in whom we have redemption
        and the forgiveness of sins.

15   You are the image of the invisible God,
        the first-born of all creation;
16   for in you all things were created,
        in heaven and on earth,
        visible and invisible,
        whether thrones or dominions
        or principalities or authorities—
        all things were created through you
        and for you.

17   You are before all things,
        and in you all things hold together.

18   You are the head of the body, the church;
        you are the beginning,

the first-born from the dead . . .
19   In you
all the fullness of God was pleased to dwell,
through you
reconciling to himself all things,
whether on earth or in heaven,
making peace by the blood of your cross.

21   And we,
were once estranged
and hostile in mind,
doing evil deeds.
22   But you have now reconciled us
in your body of flesh
by your death,
in order to present us *to your Father*
holy and blameless and irreproachable—
23   provided that we continue in the faith,
stable and steadfast,
not shifting from the hope of your gospel.

88. WHY SUFFER?

By itself, suffering is an evil. It is to be got rid of. But sufferings
come that I cannot get rid of. In addition there are crosses that I am
told to choose deliberately "as penance and mortification." But whatever the cause, whatever the pains and frustrations of life, I must
accept them in union with the cross of Christ, dedicating myself—
with him—to the ultimate happiness and welfare of the world. May

there be a progressive purification of my motives, a progressive elimination of spiritual egotism and self-seeking. I pray that as time goes on, my thoughts will become more and more centered on Christ and neighbor, less and less turned in on myself.

Col.

1:24   I rejoice in my sufferings,
         for acceptance brings grace to the world.
         In my flesh I ask to complete
         what is lacking in your afflictions, O Christ,
         for the sake of your body, that is the church ...

27   Your Father has chosen to make known
         how great ... is this mystery,
         which is you, our Lord, in us,
         our hope of glory.

28   You, therefore, we proclaim ...
         that we may present every man
         mature in you, O Christ.

29   For this we would toil,
         striving with all the energy
         which you mightily inspire within us.

         I pray for my companions in this world
2:2   that their hearts may be encouraged
         as they are knit together in love.
         May they have all the riches
         of assured understanding and knowledge ... of you
3   in whom are hid
         all the treasures of wisdom and knowledge.

89. THE QUEST OF INTEGRITY

Christians are not alone in wanting to set their minds "on things
that are above, not on things that are on earth." There is a deep-
down desire in mankind for integrity of mind and purity of body.
What I get from Christianity, therefore, is not so much the desire
as the means of realizing it. The visible water-washing of baptism
symbolizes a profound inner purification; but it is up to me to
live the new life I have been given. I have washed my hands; now
can I keep them clean?

Col.

2:6   I have received you, Jesus my Lord.
       So may I live in you,
       rooted and built up in you
       and established in the faith . . .
       and abounding in thanksgiving . . .

9   For in you
       the whole fullness of deity dwells bodily,
10   and I have come to fullness of life in you,
       who are the head of all rule and authority . . .

12   I was buried with you
       in baptism,
       in which I was also raised with you
       through faith in the working of your Father
       who raised you from the dead . . .

13   Your Father made us alive
       together with you,

having forgiven us all our trespasses,

14   having cancelled the *document of condemnation*
with its legal demands . . .
nailing it to your cross . . .

20   With you we have died
to the elemental spirits of the universe,
why then do we live
as if we still belonged to the world? . . .

3:1   We have been raised with you, O Christ.
Help us, then, seek the things that are above,
where you are,
seated at the right hand of your Father.

2   Teach us to set our minds
on things that are above,
not on things that are on earth.
3   For we have died,
and our life is hid with you in God.
But at the end of time
4   when you, our life, appear,
then we also will appear with you
in glory.

5   *Give us the strength, we pray,* to put to death
what is earthly in us:
immorality, impurity, passion,
evil desire, and covetousness . . .

7   In these we once walked ... but now
8   we want to put them all away ...

9   Help us put off the old nature
          with its practices
10   and put on the new nature,
          which is being renewed in knowledge
          after the image of its Creator.

90.   A CHOSEN PEOPLE

Christian morality is really not complicated—at least not in its fundamental guiding principles. One of its most essential principles is the brotherhood of all men in Christ; so that "here there cannot be Greek and Jew, circumcised and uncircumcised . . . slave and free man." All people are to be loved with "compassion, kindness . . . and patience." What does it profit me, then, if in church I sing every hymn with perfect pitch, if I contribute to every collection, if I show up on time for every ceremony; but if, at the same time, I admit bias in my thinking and nourish prejudice in my heart?

Col.

       You have made it abundantly clear, Lord:
3:11   Here there cannot be Greek and Jew,
       circumsised and uncircumsised,
       colored and white man,
       barbarian, Scythian, slave and free man.
       For you are all, and in all.

12   *We are called to be* your Father's chosen ones,
      holy and beloved.
      Teach us, then, compassion, kindness,
      lowliness, meekness, and patience . . .
13   and if one of us has a complaint against another,
      show us how to forgive.
      As you, Lord, have forgiven us,
      so may we also forgive one another.

14   And above all these may we put on love,
      which binds everything together
      in perfect harmony.
15   And may your peace
      rule in our hearts . . .
      And may we be thankful.

16   Let your word, O Christ,
      dwell in us richly . . .
17   so that whatever we do,
      in word or deed,
      we may do everything in your name,
      giving thanks to your Father
      through you *Jesus Christ, our Lord.*

VIII. Prayers from *Thessalonians*

AT THE HALF-WAY MARK in the first century, about 50 A.D., Paul crossed over to Europe for the first time. After founding the Church at Philippi, he moved on to Thessalonica, which was then the second city of Greece, where he made his headquarters in the home of a man named Jason. In no time there sprang up a small but flourishing Christian community—so flourishing that a jealous, hostile mob soon drove the Apostle out of the city.

Eventually Paul settled in Corinth. From there he sent Timothy back to support the Thessalonians in their new faith. Timothy returned with what was evidently an optimistic report. *I Thessalonians* is the result of Timothy's report. It was written in 51 or 52 A.D. and marks the beginning of Paul's literary career. His purpose in writing was to express his joy at the good news, to encourage the Christians to further constancy, and to answer some specific questions they had brought up. His second letter, *II Thessalonians,* followed probably within the next few months. Some more questions had been received from the North, so Paul wrote again, commenting on their difficulties and repeating his words of encouragement.

The first six of the following prayers are taken from the five chapters of *I Thessalonians.* They are reasonably repre-

184 PRAYERS FROM THESSALONIANSPRAYERS FROM THESSALONIANS

sentative of the letter as a whole. One of its major themes, however, appears only obliquely; the *parousia,* or Second Coming of Christ. As a result, the two soul-stirring prayers about death and the next life (Prayers #94 & 95) are more individualistic in tone than the original passages from which they are taken. The Christians at Thessalonica, and Paul, seem to have been very little concerned with the particular judgment—a private affair—and very much concerned with the "Day of the Lord," the last judgment—a kind of ultimate, communal liturgy. And so they pictured Christ less as a savior of individuals and more as the savior of the Church.

Unfortunately it is hard to find specific prayer passages that express this characteristic focus on the community. The emphasis in our selections, therefore, is rather more individualistic than the tone of the letter as a whole. These prayers express the gratitude of a person who has been rescued from the hopelessness of paganism (Prayer #91); Paul's reflections on his vocation as an apostle—as one officially called to the ministry of the word (Prayer #92); a Christian's view of his job, business, or profession (Prayer #93); and, in conclusion, a quick review of some of the different kinds of practical charity (Prayer #96)—concluding with the final assurance that "he who calls is faithful," and that he will never fail us.

The three prayers from *II Thessalonians* are taken, one each, from the letter's three chapters. They capture a little more of the Apostle's sense of community and Christian solidarity. The first is a warm thanksgiving for the joys of Christian friendship and for the moral encouragement that only good friends can give (Prayer #97); the second looks forward to the "Day of the Lord" for which we must arm ourselves by holding fast to "the traditions which we were taught" (Prayer #98); and the last turns again to the practical business of living, to our Christian duty of earning our daily bread "with toil and labor . . . that we may not be a burden to any of the brethren" (Prayer #99).

91.   THE LIVING GOD

In time, this is the first of the Pauline letters; so the listing here of faith, love, and hope is the first mention of this trinity of virtues in a Christian document. Why is it that I do not have as unwearied a love and as warm a hope as the Christians of Thessalonica? After all, I, too, have been saved from the worship of improbable deities like Jupiter Capitolinus, or Physical Science, or Dialectical Materialism. And I, too, have been given the wisdom to see through these dead, lifeless things, turning "from idols, to serve a living and true God."

I Thes.

> *Eternal Father, I can never thank you enough*
> *for your gift of faith, hope, and love—*
1:3 > *for calling me to a* work of faith
> and labor of love
> and steadfastness of hope
> in your Son, our Lord Jesus Christ.
>
> *For some strange reason, your love*
4 > has chosen me—

5   your gospel came to me not only in word
         but also in power and ... full conviction ...
6   with joy inspired by your Holy Spirit.

         It was your initiative and your grace
9   that turned me from idols,
         to serve you a living
         and true God,
10   and to wait for your Son from heaven,
         whom you raised from the dead,
         Jesus
         who delivers us from the wrath to come.

92. TEACHERS

In this section, Paul rejoices that he, Silvanus, and Timothy "worked
night and day that we might not burden any of you, while we
preached to you the gospel of God." But in this prayer the over-all
emphasis is less on the external way of life, and more on the inner
mind-set of the Apostle—hence of the Christian teacher. May I become less dependent on payment in money or in human gratitude.
May love so take over in my dealings with parishioners, companions,
or students that they "accept [what I say] not as the word of men
but as . . . the word of God."

I Thes.

2:2   *We ask for* courage to declare *the Good News*
         in the face of great opposition ...

4   By you we have been entrusted with the gospel,
     so we must speak, not to please men,
     but to please you
     who test our hearts.

     O, give us the honesty
5   never to use words of flattery ...
6   nor to seek glory from men ...
     nor to make demands as apostles of your Son.
8   *Teach us, rather,* to share with our brothers
     not only your gospel, O God,
     but also our own selves,
9   *ready if need be* to work night and day,
     that we might not burden any of them
     while we preach to them your gospel.

10   How holy and righteous and blameless
     ought to be our behavior to all believers.
11   *Help us to realize*
     how like a father with his children,
     we should exhort each one of them
     and encourage them
12   and charge them to lead a life worthy of you
     who are calling them
     into your own kingdom and glory.

13   When these men receive your word, O God,
     which they hear from us,
     may they accept it
     not as the word of men

but as—what it really is—your word,
which is at work in all believers.

93.   LOVE IN BUSINESS

Perhaps we do not pray enough about our job and business dealings with neighbors and fellow citizens. (A variant translation
would apply the text to marriage rather than to business—but
surely both are valid subjects for prayer.) Love must show itself
in act, above all in those familiar acts of the working day that
absorb such a large part of our energies.

I Thes.

3:12   O Lord, make us increase and abound
            in love to one another
            and to all men . . .
13   so that you may establish our hearts
            unblamable in holiness
            before our God and Father
            at *the final day* of your coming, Lord Jesus,
            with all your saints.

            *A true Christian, you have said, must be honest
            and reliable on the job,*
6   and not defraud his brother in business,
            because you, Lord, are an avenger
            in all these things . . .
8   Therefore whoever disregards this

disregards not man but your Father in heaven,
who gives his Holy Spirit to us . . .

9   We have been taught by your Father
       to love one another . . .
10   May we do so more and more,
11   and aspire to live quietly,
       to mind our own affairs,
       and to work with our hands . . . so that
12   we may command the respect of outsiders
       and be dependent on nobody,
       but only on you, our Lord and our God.

94. DEATH AND ETERNITY

For so many in our own age, as in Paul's, the only certain time is
the present. And any frantic effort to enjoy this fleeting present "before it is too late" is self-condemned to be self-defeating. So it is
that today the bright, eternal certitudes of Christianity stand out
ever so clearly against the sable backdrop of existentialist despair. If
my mind and heart were only more in tune with reality, with what
warm hopes should I look forward to the time when "we shall
be caught up . . . in the clouds to meet the Lord."

I Thes.

       Teach me to understand death, O Lord,
4:13   *and not to be* ignorant
       concerning those who are asleep.

That I may not grieve
as others do who have no hope!

14   I believe that you died and rose again.
Even so, through you,
your Father will bring *together in heaven*
those who have fallen asleep.

Again, you have assured me
that at the end of the world
15   those of us who are alive,
who are left until your coming, O Lord,
shall not precede those who have fallen asleep.
16   For you yourself will descend from heaven
with a cry of command,
with the archangel's call,
and with the sound of the trumpet of God.
And the dead will rise first;
17   then we who are alive, who are left,
shall be caught up together with them
in the clouds to meet you, our Lord;
and so we shall always be with you.

Lord, in times of bereavement,
18   help us to comfort one another
with these words.

95. PIE IN THE SKY

If I were more fully conscious of the world to come, I should be more, not less, energetic in the world that is here. Christians have been accused of waiting comfortably for "pie in the sky when we die," of passively praying for rain when they ought to be actively building a dam. To the extent that the charge is true, it is a measure not of our Christian faith but of our lack of it—and of a corresponding lack of vital hope and energetic love.

I Thes.

O God, help me to keep in mind
5:2 and to know well
that the day of the Lord
will come like a thief in the night.
3 When we say: "There is peace and security,"
then sudden destruction will come upon us ...
and there will be no escape.

I ask to keep this in mind,
but I pray not to be terrified by it.
4 *After all* we are not in darkness
for that day to surprise us like a thief.
No, thanks to your Son, our Savior,
5 we are all sons of light
and sons of the day;
we are not of the night or of darkness.

6 So then let us not sleep,
as others do,

but let us keep awake
and be sober.

7   For those who sleep sleep at night,
        and those who get drunk are drunk at night.

8   But, since we belong to the day,
        let us be sober,
        and put on the breastplate of faith
        and of love,
        and for a helmet the hope of salvation.

        May we always keep this truth in mind—
9   You have not destined us for wrath,
        but to obtain salvation
        through our Lord Jesus Christ,
10   who died for us
        so that whether we wake or sleep
        we might live
        with him.

96.   LOVE AND INITIATIVE

Christ, man and God, is the Father's supreme gift to mankind. In one way or another the whole of this epistle is about God's initiative in salvation history, his choice of me, his free gift, his "grace." My response to this divine love must be human love—so that nobody "repays evil for evil." Instead, Christians are "to do good to one another . . . to encourage the faint-hearted, help the weak, and be patient with all."

I Thes.

5:11   *Help us, Lord,* to encourage one another
and build one another up ...

13   and be at peace among ourselves.

14   *Teach us to* admonish the idle,
encourage the faint-hearted,
help the weak,
and be patient with them all.

15   *May we never* repay evil for evil,
but always seek to do good to one another
and to all.
In a word, may we learn how to

16   rejoice always,

17   pray constantly,

18   and give thanks in all circumstances;
for this is your will, O God,
in Christ Jesus ...

23   We ask you, our Father, God of peace,
to sanctify us wholly.
May our spirit and soul and body
be kept sound and blameless
for the coming of your Son, Jesus Christ.

24   *We firmly believe*
that you who have called us
are faithful,
and that you will *never fail us.*

97.   CHRIST IN MY BROTHERS

What a difference it makes to grow up among people who love one another! Tragically, as I am well aware, there are whole areas of the globe where an act of selfless love still elicits the suspicious question: "Wonder what he's trying to soften me up for?" And equally tragically, in our own once-Christian part of the world a generation of children is growing up with much the same attitude, children who have seen far too little of the love of Christ in their parents, teachers, and guides. In contrast, what warm strength it gives me to experience in my brothers the reality of Christ's love.

II Thes.

> *As members of this your Christian family,*
>
> *1:3*   we are bound to give thanks
> to your Father in heaven
> always . . . as is fitting,
> because our faith is growing abundantly,
> and the love
> of every one of us for one another
> is increasing—
>
> *4*   *especially where there are* persecutions
> and afflictions which we are enduring.
>
>
> *5*   *We pray that* we may be made worthy
> of the kingdom of your Father,
> for which we are suffering.
>
> *6*   Since indeed he deems it just
> to repay with affliction

those who afflict us,

7   *I know that eventually he will* grant rest
to us who are afflicted,
when you, Lord Jesus, are revealed from heaven
with the mighty angels
in flaming fire ...

10   You will come on that day
to be glorified in your saints ...

11   To this end
I always pray that our Father
may make us worthy of his call,
and may fulfill every good resolve and work of faith
by his power.

12   May your name, O Lord,
be glorified in us,
and we in you,
according to the grace of our Father in heaven
and of you, Lord Jesus Christ.

98.   BEFORE THE END

The early Christians were very much aware of the "Day of the Lord," Christ's coming in victory at the end of time. May I, with Saint Paul, recognize in this second coming the ultimate, triumphant vindication both of Christ's work and of mine. With this in mind, I will "stand firm and hold to the traditions" I have learned, confident in the outcome, no matter how unscrupulous the opposition, no matter how virulent "the mystery of lawlessness [that] is already at work."

II Thes.

	I look forward to the end of time
2:1	*and to* your coming, Lord Jesus Christ,
	and our assembling to meet you.
2	*But I pray* not to be shaken in mind or excited
	either by spirit or by word or by letter . . .
	to the effect that *this end of our world,*
	this "day of the Lord," has come . . .
7	*Your Apostle says that* the mystery of lawlessness
	is already at work,
	and that eventually, at the end of time,
8	the lawless one will be revealed,
	and you, Lord Jesus, will slay him
	with the breath of your mouth
	and destroy him by your appearing.
9	*I know, too, that* the coming of the lawless one—
	by the activity of Satan—
	will be with all power
	and with pretended signs and wonders,
10	and with all wicked deception
	for those who are to perish
	because they refused to love the truth . . .

13   We are bound
        to give thanks to your Father always . . .
        because you have chosen us from the beginning
        to be saved,
        through sanctification by the Spirit
        and belief in the truth.

14   To this you have called us through the gospel
        so that we may obtain your glory, Lord Jesus.
15   *Help us* then to stand firm
        and hold to the traditions which we were taught.
16   *We ask you,* Lord Jesus Christ,
        and you, God our Father,
        who loved us and gave us eternal comfort
        and good hope through grace,
17   to *strengthen* our hearts and establish them
        in every good work and word.

99.   THE JOB TO BE DONE

In the Greek of verse 11 there is a play on words that might be translated "not busy but busybodies." When I am not really immersed in the job to be done, how quickly do I become just this, a busybody: a religious administrator who insists on making all the decisions for his congregation; a spiritual enthusiast who tries to be in on everyone's comings and goings; a parent, foreman, or employer who insists on giving minute, detailed instructions to all

who are under him. But my job is Christ's. If I knew this and were
really busy at it, I would have no time to be a busybody.

II Thes.

       It is my privilege to be a witness to the gospel.
3:1   May your word, O Lord,
        speed on and triumph ...
2   May we be delivered from wicked and evil men.

       I know, but I need to be constantly reminded
3   that you, Lord, are faithful;
        that you will strengthen us
        and guard us from evil ...
5   Direct our hearts, *we pray,*
        to the love of your Father.

       Help us to do a day's work for a day's pay,
6   to keep away from any who are living in idleness ...
8   and not to eat any one's bread without paying,
        but with toil and labor
        to work night and day—
        that we may not be a burden
        to any of the brethren.

11   *Keep us from wanting to* live in idleness,
        mere busybodies,
        not doing any work.
12   *Give us the energy* to do our work
        in quietness
        and to earn our own living.

13   *May we never* grow weary in well-doing ...
16   So may you, O Lord of peace,
        yourself give us peace
        at all times
        and in all ways.

IX. Prayers from the Pastoral Epistles

THE SO-CALLED PASTORAL EPISTLES (polished, it would seem, and edited from St. Paul's original, hasty instructions) are letters of pastoral advice written by a pastor to pastors—to Timothy at Ephesus, and to Titus on the Island of Crete. They were intended both for the recipients, to encourage them in their work for the Lord, and for their respective churches, to instruct the faithful and to reinforce the authority of the two bishops Paul had appointed.

Titus and *Philemon*

In the first of these letters Paul sets out to instruct Titus on specific matters of church discipline and on the necessity of appointing worthy ministers of the gospel. At the same time he wants the Christian faithful on the Island of Crete to see what confidence he places in his representative and how close is the bond between the Apostle and his vicar.

The following prayers flow from Paul's instruction about the personal qualities that an individual must have if he is to be appointed to a position of authority in the Church (Prayer #100), and about the attitude that Christians should have towards one another, especially towards those of different occupation or ability level (Prayers #101,102). Lastly he sets down the doctrinal foundation of both charity and authority, namely the freedom of all God's gifts to mankind (Prayer #102).

The warm, little two-page note to Philemon is a different kind of letter. It is not considered one of the pastoral epistles, and is included in this chapter only because space was conveniently on hand. Our one prayer from it (Prayer #103) pretty well summarizes the letter: Philemon should see in Onesimus not his run-away slave, but a dear brother in Christ. This Christian transformation of Philemon's thinking should then become the pattern for our own putting on of the mind of Christ.

I and II Timothy

In these two "open letters" to a minister of the gospel, Paul is anxious to strengthen his "beloved son's" position in the Church, assuring both Timothy and his flock that a pastor's youthfulness is no hindrance to the apostolate, that he must forget about his personal limitations and think rather of the grace of Christ and the power he received "when the elders laid their hands upon" him (Prayer #108).

Evidently the main lines of Christian doctrine had been well formulated by the time Paul wrote these letters. There is an emphasis, therefore, on preserving sound doctrine and passing it on as part of the deposit of faith. Our prayers, however, concentrate rather on the splendor of the Christian vision (Prayers #107,109), on the corresponding response of a spiritually minded husband in a Christian home (Prayer #106), and on the charity, patience, and forgiveness that is expected of all Christian (Prayers #104,110).

II Timothy is the last of Paul's letters. If he wrote anything else, it has not come down to us. These, then, are the Apostle's last recorded words before his death—before his "going home" as he called it. Strangely, the poignant final chapter of this letter reads almost like a deliberate last testament, witnessing as it does to God's eternal fidelity (Prayer #116) and to Paul's own longing for the prize, "the crown of righteousness," that is waiting for him (Prayer #115).

Looking back on the long, work-filled days of his missionary journeys, Paul sees their brutal hardship and suffering against the background of Christ's ever-present strength and encouragement (Prayer #112). There is still time to sound yet another warning against those who preserve all the outward "form of religion [when at heart they are] denying the power of it" (Prayer #114). This warning against false teachers is as firm and uncompromising as ever; yet it is the same writer who insists that "the Lord's servant must . . . be kindly to everyone, an apt teacher, forbearing, and correcting his opponents with gentleness" (Prayer #113).

Could it be that, as he wrote these words, the Apostle's great, unforgetting mind flashed back a picture from his youth when, before that transforming vision of Christ on the road to Damascus, he subscribed to a far more drastic way of dealing with error? Could it be, too, that he still remembered Stephen's last words when "the witnesses laid down their garments at the feet of a young man named Saul"? For the words were an echo of his Master's prayer: "Lord, do not hold this sin against them."

100.   GOD'S HOUSE

On the Island of Crete, far from Paul and the other apostles, Titus *was the church*. People looked to him, to his life and to his words, and then measured for themselves the truth and value of Christianity. There are members of my family, people where I work, citizens in my community who are equally far—in spirit, if not in body—from the official teachers of the Church. In their eyes, I, too, am the Church. At my own level, like the Bishop Titus at his, I am a steward of God's house. May I be preserved from all delusions about my ability to look after it without the Owner's assistance, advice, and constant encouragement.

Titus

1:1   I am a servant of God the Father
           and your apostle, Jesus Christ,
           to further the faith of your elect
           and their knowledge of the truth
2   *and their* hope of eternal life
           which your Father, who never lies, promised
           ages ago.

           It is my privilege to offer this truth
           and this life of yours to the world
3   through the preaching
           with which I have been entrusted.
4   *May we all come to share* grace and peace
           from our Father
           and from you, Christ Jesus our Savior . . .

7   As your steward, I must be blameless;
      I must not be arrogant
      or quick-tempered or a drunkard or violent
      or greedy for gain.
8   *Show me how to be* hospitable,
      a lover of goodness,
      master of myself,
      upright, holy, and self-controlled.

9   *Help me to* hold firm to the sure word
      as taught,
      so that I may be able
      to give instruction in sound doctrine
      and also to confute those who contradict it.
      Above all, may I never
16   profess to know you, my God,
      but deny it by my deeds.

101. SPIRITUAL HUNGER

Christ has put in our hands a pearl of great price, a treasure that
rust and moth will not consume, a spiritual bank account that
leaves us, "awaiting our blessed hope, the appearing of the glory
of our great God and Savior." But wealth involves responsibility as
well as privilege. What am I doing to distribute the superabundance
of this wealth to the spiritually underdeveloped sectors of my
world? And how can I develop a sense of urgency in the task,
sufficient to counteract my natural torpor and laziness?

Titus

2:7   *Help me to* show myself in all respects
        a model of good deeds.
        I ask that my teaching show integrity,
8   gravity, and sound speech
        that cannot be censured,
        so that an opponent may be put to shame,
        having nothing evil to say of us . . .
10   In everything
        may I adorn your doctrine, my God and my Savior.

11   Your grace, O God, has appeared
        for the salvation of all men,
12   training us to renounce irreligion
        and worldly passions,
        and to live sober, upright, and godly lives
        in this world,
13   awaiting our blessed hope,
        the appearing of your glory.

        It is you we await,
        our great God and Savior Jesus Christ,
14   who gave yourself for us
        to redeem us from all iniquity
        and to purify for yourself a people of your own.
        Help us, we pray, to be zealous for good deeds.

102.   AWARENESS OF GRACE

Myself and all that I have is God's gift. Sin alone is my own to boast of. If I am dissatisfied with my talents, I am dissatisfied with God. And if I despise the culture or talents of another, I am again despising God. It is "not because of deeds done by us" that the Son of God came down to earth to give us a "washing of regeneration and renewal in the Holy Spirit." No, all is gift. If I could get even a speck of this realization, with what "perfect courtesy [would I treat] all men," never looking down on people of different social status, or insulting them because of their nationality, religion or race.

Titus

3:1   You remind us, Lord,
to be submissive
to rulers and authorities,
to be obedient,
to be ready for any honest work,

2   to speak evil of no one,
to avoid quarreling, to be gentle,
and to show perfect courtesy
toward all men.

*But how we try to feel and act superior
to others, forgetting our own past,
insisting on deference and respect,*

3   when we ourselves were once foolish,
disobedient, led astray,
slaves to various passions and pleasures,
passing our days in malice and envy,

hated by men and hating one another.

It was then that we experienced
4   your goodness and loving kindness,
     O God our Savior.
5   You saved us,
     not because of deeds done by us . . .
     but in virtue of your own mercy.

     Our washing of regeneration
     and renewal in the Holy Spirit
6   you poured out upon us richly
     through Jesus Christ our savior,
7   so that we might be justified by his grace
     and become heirs,
     in hope of eternal life.

103.   AS WE FORGIVE OTHERS

In this warmly personal, two-page letter, Paul asks his friend
Philemon to receive back his run-away slave, Onesimus, to forgive
him and to welcome him as a dear brother in Christ—a timely
reminder for all who have experienced class prejudice and racial
antagonism. (More liberty has been taken in transposing this prayer
than the others, changing persons and changing the background
from the problem of slavery to that of personal offense. In the con-
text Paul is speaking of his own love for Onesimus. But since Paul's
love is after all only a reflection of his Divine Master's, we have

transposed this one prayer in such a way that Paul's words become
Christ's.) What an increase of joy would come to my day, and how
much richer would be my dealings with others if, with Philemon, I
could control the irregular pulse of my own jealous and resentful
heart by getting it to beat in harmony with the heart of Christ—if,
in Paul's favorite phrase, I could live *in Christ*.

Philemon

1:3   May grace be ours and peace
from God our Father
and from you, Lord Jesus Christ.

6   *And may we be able to* share our faith
with others
and promote the knowledge of all the good
that is ours in you, O Christ.

Lord, you know how much I dislike   X   .

11   Formerly he was useless, *unkind and hateful* to me.
But now *I want to see that* he is useful to you ...

12   and you are sending him back to me.

Teach me how to forgive—for in him
you are sending me your very heart.
I know that you won't force him on me

14   for you prefer to do nothing without my consent
in order that my goodness
may not be by compulsion
but of my own free will.

15   Perhaps this is why
      he was *allowed to hurt me* for a while,
      that I might have him back for ever,
16   no longer as a *sinner*
      but as a beloved brother ... in you, O Lord.
17   *Teach me* to receive him
      as I would receive you ...
25   May your grace, O Lord Jesus Christ,
      be with my spirit.

104.   PATTERN FOR PARDON

How thoroughly have I experienced God's mercy—I, who was once so thoughtless, so self-centered, so indifferent to his love. Now he has gone beyond mercy and forgiveness, and has "appointed me to his service." May I learn from his patience towards me what it means to be patient towards others, so that through me they, too, may come to discover him "for eternal life."

I Timothy

1:12   I thank you
      who have given me strength,
      Christ Jesus my Lord.
      Now you have appointed me to your service.
13   Though I formerly blasphemed
      and persecuted and insulted you,
      still I received mercy ...

14   Your grace, O Lord,
      overflowed for me
      with the faith and love that are in you.

15   *How well I know that* the saying is sure
      and worthy of full acceptance,
      that you, Christ Jesus,
      came into the world to save sinners.

16   *Perhaps* I received mercy for this reason,
      that in me . . . you might display
      your perfect patience, as an example
      to those who are to believe in you
      for eternal life.

17   To you, king of ages,
      immortal, invisible,
      the only God,
      be honor and glory for ever and ever.
      Amen.

105.   FOR PRESIDENTS AND RULERS

Political life is a life of crisis and temptation, but it is also a life
of opportunity for creative improvement and for Christian concern. If only more statesmen and politicians saw themselves as in-
struments of God's plan for the world! For my part, I must at least
pray for all those "who are in high positions," that they may have
the conviction and the courage to lead our world towards its

ultimate common good—toward that temporal community where men will be more able to grow in virtue and truth.

1 Timothy

Lord, teach me to serve you as you deserve,
1:18 that I may wage the good warfare,
19 holding faith
   and a good conscience ...
2:1 First of all, *I want to offer* supplications,
   prayers, intercessions, and thanksgivings
   for all men,
   but especially for presidents and rulers
2 and for all who are in high positions,
   that we may lead a quiet and peaceable life.
3 *You have told me that this prayer* is good,
   and that it is acceptable in your sight,
   my God and Savior.
4 For you desire all men to be saved
   and to come to the knowledge of the truth.

106. CHRIST IN THE FAMILY

In the daily routine of life there is nothing that has to be wasted. Christ is present always. All that I do—sin alone excepted—can witness to his redemptive concern for mankind. May his love be able to reach out, through me, to my family and companions; may his "great confidence" find entrance into the marketplace in my person.

I Timothy

> *Both at home with the children and away on the job*
> *I must bear witness to your truth,*

2:5   that there is one God
    and one mediator between God and men,
    you, the man Christ Jesus.

6   You gave yourself as a ransom for all;

7   and I am your preacher and apostle . . .
    a teacher of the people in faith and truth.

> *With your help and encouragement, I want*

3:2   to be above reproach,
    married only once . . .
    hospitable,
    an apt teacher . . .

3   not quarrelsome, and no lover of money.

4   Help me to manage my own household well,
    keeping the children submissive
    and respectful . . .

13   *Above all, give me* great confidence
    in the faith
    which is in you Christ Jesus.

107.   MYSTERY OF FAITH

Faith for Paul—and faith for me, I hope—is more than a verbal statement of belief, more than a mental assent to the naked truth of God's existence, more than a warm feeling of subjective confidence. It is the fully accepting openness of created man, body and soul, to the reality of his Creator God. It is my total response both to Christ "manifested in the flesh," and to Christ "taken up in glory." As such it is a response that embraces both the immediate pleasures God has created for me in this world and the holiness to which he is calling me in the next.

I Timothy

3:16   Great indeed, I confess,
               is the mystery of our religion:
               God manifested in the flesh,
               vindicated in the Spirit,
               seen by angels,
               preached among the nations,
               believed on in the world,
               taken up in glory.

               The joys of life—music and feasting,
               friendship and marriage—everything
4:3   you created
               to be received with thanksgiving
               by those who believe and know the truth.
4   For everything created by you is good
               and nothing is to be rejected
               if it is received with thanksgiving—

5   for then it is consecrated
by your word, O God, and by prayers.

Father in heaven, help me
6   to be a good minister of Christ Jesus,
nourished on the words of the faith
and of the good doctrine which I have followed.

May I learn to drive from my life
7   *all superstitions* and silly myths,
and to train myself in godliness.
8   For while bodily training is of some value,
godliness is of value in every way,
as it holds promise for the present life
and also for the life to come.

10   To this end may we toil and strive,
because we have our hope set on you,
the living God,
on you, the Savior of all men.

108.   YOUTH AND AUTHORITY

It was natural for the churches of Asia Minor to look to the church
at Ephesus for leadership. But it was not so natural that the church
at Ephesus should look for leadership to a young presbyter by the
name of Timothy. Saint Paul wrote this letter, therefore, to remind
both Timothy and his fellow Christians that authority in the Church

is founded not on personal charism but on the authority of Christ.
In doing so, he gives renewed resolution and an increase of courage
to all who are young—whether in age or in experience—and who
find themselves thrust into positions of responsibility in the Church.

I Timothy

> *Lord, show me how to act so that*

4:12   no one will despise my youth.
     May I set the believers an example
     in speech and conduct,
     in love, in faith, and in purity.

> *With your divine assistance*

13   I will attend to the public reading of scripture,
     to preaching, and to teaching.

14   May I not neglect the gift I have,
     which was given me by prophetic utterance
     when the elders laid their hands upon me.

15   May I practice these duties,
     devoting myself to them ...

16   and take heed to myself
     and to my teaching.
     For by so doing I will save
     both myself
     and my hearers.

109. LOVE OF MONEY

The progressive dechristianization of our Western world can be measured by our growing "love of money" and by a corresponding multiplication of "senseless and hurtful desires." *Love* of money is a grasping thing that makes us less and less willing to allocate a substantial proportion of our wealth—not only of our surplus—to the underdeveloped countries with their suffering children and with their anguished, but illiterate and economically helpless, parents. So it is man's selfish unconcern that is now threatening to plunge the whole world "into ruin and destruction."

I Timothy

6:7   We brought nothing into the world,
        and we cannot take anything out;

8   but if we have food and clothing,
        with these, *O God, teach us to* be content.

9   Those who desire to be rich
        fall into temptation,
        into a snare,
        into many senseless and hurtful desires
        that plunge men into ruin and destruction.

10   For the love of money, *you have warned me,*
        is the root of all evils;
        it is through this craving that some
        have wandered away from the faith
        and pierced their hearts with many pangs.

11   *May I learn* to shun all this;
          to aim at righteousness, godliness, and faith,
          love, steadfastness, and gentleness.
          With the stimulus of your grace, I will
12   fight the good fight of the faith;
          and take hold of the eternal life
          to which I was called . . .
14   You have charged me
          to keep *doing my work*
          unstained and free from reproach
          until the appearing of our Lord Jesus Christ.

          I believe that his full truth and his goodness
15   will be made manifest
          at the proper time
          by you, our blessed and only Sovereign,
          King of kings and Lord of lords.
16   You alone have immortality,
          and you dwell in unapproachable light
          so that no man has ever seen
          or can see you.
          To you be honor and eternal domination.
          Amen.

110. RICHES THAT DO NOT FAIL

St. Paul has just warned against a grasping love of money. I can see for myself the progressive destruction of personality that this "love" effects. But I will never be able to exorcise myself of its spirit unless I find a more powerful spirit to take its place. Repeated warnings about the dangers of materialism will have no lasting effect on me until I acquire a mature, supernatural vision of man, of the primacy of spirit, and of the wisdom of Christian love.

I Timothy

6:17
Those of us who are rich
in this world,
rich in money, education, or talent,
need your help not to be haughty,
nor to set our hopes
on uncertain *and ultimately disappointing goals*
but on you, our God,
who richly furnish us
with everything
to enjoy.

18
Teach us how to do good,
to be rich in good deeds,
liberal and generous,
19
thus laying up for ourselves
a good foundation for the future,
so that we may take hold of that *real* life
which is life indeed.

20   *Help us to* guard
        what has been entrusted to us;
        and to avoid the godless chatter
        and contradictions
        of what is falsely called knowledge.

111.   A SPIRIT OF POWER

Power was given Timothy with the imposition of hands. Now it is
up to him to *use* that power. Sacramental grace is not a magic force;
it "works" only with human cooperation. It has to be fanned into
flame. Since all of us have received a share in the priesthood of
Christ—each according to his position in the Church which is his
body—Paul's prayer for Timothy becomes a prayer for every baptized, or ordained Christian.

II Timothy

        At my own level, I am your apostle
1:1   by the will of your Father
        according to the promise of the life
        which is in you, Christ Jesus.

2   *I have received* grace, mercy, and peace
        from your Father
        and from you, Jesus my Lord.

6   *Help me, I pray,* to rekindle
        the divine gift that is within me
        through the laying on of hands;

7   for you did not give me a spirit of timidity
            but a spirit of power
            and love
            and self-control.

8   I do not want to be ashamed then
            of testifying to you, my Lord,
            and I ask to be strong enough
            to take my share of suffering for the gospel . . .

9   Your Father saved us
            and called us with a holy calling,
            not in virtue of our works
            but in virtue of his own purpose
            and the grace which he gave us
            in you, Christ Jesus, ages ago . . .

10   You abolished death
            and brought life and immortality.
            And of this, your Good News,
11   I have been appointed
            a preacher and apostle and teacher . . .

12   I know whom I have believed
            and I am sure
            that you are able
            to guard . . . what has been entrusted to me.
13   *Enable me to* follow
            the pattern of sound words
            which I have heard from you.

Help me to grow in the faith and love
which are in you, Christ Jesus,
14   and to guard the truth
that has been entrusted to me
by your Holy Spirit
who dwells within us.

112.   ATHLETE OF CHRIST

If I am doing the work of Christ I have nothing to fear, for his
love is above and beside and within me. But I will have much to
endure: No race, no crown; no plowing, no harvest; no death with
Christ now, no life with him hereafter.

II Timothy

2:1   I will be strong
in the grace that is in you, my Lord ...

3   I will take my share of suffering
as a good soldier ...

5   An athlete, *you have reminded me,*
is not crowned
unless he competes according to the rules.

6   It is the hard-working farmer
who ought to have the first share of the crops.
These are your own examples, Lord,

7   *and I ask you* to grant me understanding ...

9   The word of God is not fettered.
10   Therefore I *am willing to* endure anything
     for the sake of *your brothers and mine*
     that they may obtain your salvation
     which ... goes with eternal glory ...

11   If we have died with you
     we shall also live with you.
12   If we endure
     we shall also reign with you.
     But if we deny you
     you also will deny us ...
13   for you cannot deny yourself.

113.   TOLERANCE

Christ is not proclaimed in loud words and bitter argument. I am
called to be an apostle, not a debater; to give an example of "love
and peace," not of power and domination. The redeeming presence
of Christ is always felt as a gentle hand, correcting with love that
all may "repent and come to know the truth."

II Timothy
       Lord, I want to do my best
2:15   to present myself to your Father
       as ... a workman who has no need to be ashamed,
       rightly handling the word of truth.

22   *I pray for strength to* shun youthful passions
            and so aim at righteousness,
            faith, love, and peace,
            along with *all those friends of yours*
            who call upon you from a pure heart.

23   May I have nothing to do with stupid,
            senseless controversies . . .
            that only breed quarrels.

24   For your servant, O Lord,
            must not be quarrelsome
            but kindly to every one,
            an apt teacher,
            forbearing,

25   and correcting his opponents with gentleness . . .
            that they may repent
            and come to know the truth.

114. THE MEANING OF RELIGION

Now that I have turned from the mere outward "form of religion" to its inner meaning, I find that it is anything but an opiate of the people. Religion is not a dreamlike escape from the world; it is the hard confrontation of created man and uncreated reality—of darkness and light, of love and persecution. Fortunately there is a partial road map to guide my searching steps, the scriptures which are divinely inspired "for teaching . . . and for training in righteousness."

II Timothy

Lord, I confess that I have been
3:2   in love with self,
       a lover of money,
       proud, arrogant, abusive ... ungrateful ...
4   swollen with conceit,
       a lover of pleasure rather than a lover of God,
5   holding the *outward* form of religion
       but denying the power of it.

But now I am trying to lead a better life.
12   And I accept the fact that all who desire
       to live a godly life in you, Christ Jesus,
       will be persecuted.

14   But in spite of this I hope to continue
       in what I have learned
       and have firmly believed,
       knowing from whom I learned it,
15   and having your sacred writings ...
       to instruct me for salvation ...
16   For all scripture
       is inspired by you, my God,
       and is profitable for teaching,
       for reproof, for correction,
       and for training in righteousness.
17   Help me, Lord, to be a man of God,
       complete,
       and equipped for every good work.

115.   WITNESS TO UNBELIEVERS

For the first time in history we are confronted with a widespread
and positive rejection of God. Modern man, unable to live in a
theological vacuum, has "wandered into myths," turning to pseudo-
science, to Marxist dialectics, even to astrology. And I personally
must accept a large share of the blame for this tragedy, for I have
witnessed so inadequately to "his splendor and wonder." O, may
the rest of my days be the beginning of a new witness—of one that
will be at once more adequate, more eloquent, and more persuasive.

II Timothy

> *In fear and in hope and in love, I stand*
4:1   in the presence of your Eternal Father
> and of you, Christ Jesus,
> who are to judge the living and the dead.

> *I know that you have commissioned me*
2   to preach the word,
> to be urgent in season and out of season,
> to convince, rebuke, and exhort,
> and to be unfailing in patience and in teaching.

> For the time *you foretold*
3   *seems to be at hand,*
> when people do not endure sound teaching,
> but having itching ears
> they accumulate for themselves
> teachers to suit their own likings;

4   and they turn away from listening to the truth
       and wander into myths.

5   As for me,
       may I always be steady,
       endure suffering,
       do the work of an evangelist,
       and fulfill my ministry.

6   *For soon, I know* the time of my departure
       will come.
       May I then be able to say, with your Apostle,
7   "I have fought the good fight,
       I have finished the race,
       I have kept the faith.
8   Henceforth there is laid up for me
       the crown of righteousness,
       which you, Lord, . . . will award to me
       on that Day,
       and not only to me
       but also to all who have loved your appearing."

116.   ALONE, WITH GOD

This prayer is from Paul's last recorded words. It is a poignant last testament in which he looks back over the long course of his life and is reminded of the evil that is in man: the hostility of enemies, the inconstancy of friends. But what is man's weakness when it is

submerged in, and surrounded by, the strength of God? What does
it matter that I am "deserted" by everybody, if only Christ is at my
side, the Savior who "will rescue me from every evil and save me
for his heavenly kingdom?"

II Timothy

O God, you have been with me in my trials

4:16   when no one took my part,
      when all deserted me—
       May it not be charged against them!

17   *Always* you stood by me
      and gave me strength
      to proclaim the word fully,
      that all the people might hear it.

I have learned to trust in you, my Lord,
and I am fully confident

18   that you will rescue me
      from every evil
      and save me for your heavenly kingdom.
      To you be the glory
      for ever and ever.   Amen.

Topical Index*

* *Italics* refer to prayers of gratitude and joy, *roman type* to prayers for times of worry or concern.

5. DEALING WITH MONEY

God has been good to us: no one is in the hospital: we've eaten all week: the kids have warm clothes. We have enough.

13 16 51 70 89 95 100 110

Bills to be paid; the car has broken down; the water heater doesn't heat. . . .

4 9 11 18 25 47 48 56 80 83 115

We have more than enough: enough to share, enough to make others happy too.

1 12 30 43 52 53 60 82 92 97 109

6. GETTING ON AT WORK

Oh, why did I ever get into this?

3 8 24 31 34 42 53 60 71 73 93 98 99 109 116

A bunch of incompetents!

40 49 54 77 84 90 96 102 104 112

At last there's something I can do well.

1 19 66 75 85 105 107 110 111 113

I've been passed over; the boss doesn't appreciate me.

5 9 25 35 47 57 74 82 97 108

At last, we're all pulling together.

6 33 46 72 93 95 100

Hasn't he got anything to do? Why can't he waste someone else's time?

12 58 64 68 70 79 88 90 99 101 103 113

Index for Prayers of Personal Concern

7. The world is passing me by. *How helpless I am.* PRAYER FOR FAITH.

   3 6 54 55 60 82 91

8. Another present from Above. *How good* is God. PRAYER OF THANKS.

   5 16 36 68 71 91 97 107 116

9. Where are all my friends? Why must I feel so *rejected?* PRAYER FOR HOPE.

   9 42 45 49 69 86 94 105 113 115

10. I'm becoming smug and *complacent.* PRAYER FOR HUMILITY.

    11 22 24 26 39 66 70 74 81 99 100 102

11. I've been so restless and *irritable* of late. PRAYER FOR PATIENCE.

    3 6 13 25 57 67 77 114

12. Lord, help me to be *sorry for my sins.* PRAYER FOR SORROW.

    2 5 7 22 26 33 61 70 81 87 88 103 104 114

13. Lord, I want *to receive you* into my heart and life. COMMUNION PRAYER.

    9 12 20 23 34 35 41 46 50 80 82 85 96 107 109

14. *Discouragement:* Nothing works out right. What can I do? PRAYER FOR STRENGTH.

    39 51 54 57 78 89 93

15. If I could only bury all these *feelings of dislike,* hostility, jealousy, and resentment. PRAYER FOR UNITY.

    12 14 17 21 35 36 37 65 66 71 72 73 74 76 79 83 96 102 103 110 112 113

16. I'm concerned about discrimination and *race prejudice.* PRAYER FOR JUSTICE.

    10 13 19 30 34 38 50 52 56 62 72 80 90 104
    111 115

17. May there be a new flowering of *Christian love,* as well among ourselves as among the nations of the world. PRAYER FOR PEACE.

    3 12 17 24 31 45 48 54 58 63 71 73 95 101
    105 109

Index for the Spiritual Exercises of a Retreat